A DREAM COME TRUE:

ROBERT HUGMAN and
SAN ANTONIO'S RIVER WALK

Robert Hugman's own blueprints were used in 1988 to construct an unbuilt portion of arched stone wall he originally envisioned along Crockett Street, making yet another part of his dream come true.

by

VERNON G. ZUNKER

REVISED EDITION

Cover photo courtesy of La Mansion del Rio Hotel

THE AUTHOR

Vernon G. Zunker

Vernon G. Zunker, a college professor and psychologist, was born 30 miles east of San Antonio near Seguin.

He received a Bachelor's degree from Texas Lutheran College, a Master's degree from Trinity University, a Doctoral degree from the University of Houston, and completed a residency in clinical psychology at the University of Texas Medical School in Galveston.

He has written numerous articles and two college textbooks, now in their fourth editions.

For several years, he and his wife, Rosalie, have enjoyed an apartment located on the Big Bend section of the San Antonio River Walk.

Many of the pages in this book were written in their apartment and on their balcony, from which one can observe the activities along the river.

David Anthony Richelieu Photo

A Dream Come True:
Robert Hugman and
San Antonio's River Walk
Revised Edition

Printed by the GraphicShop
1012 San Pedro Avenue
San Antonio, Texas 78212-5496
Phone 210 226-2117

Bound by Universal Bookbindery, Inc.
1200 N. Colorado Street
San Antonio, Texas 78207
Phone 210 734-9502

Designed, produced, printed and manufactured
in its entirety in the United States of America

CONTENTS

ACKNOWLEDGMENTS

This book -- and its revision -- are an expression of my admiration for Robert H.H. Hugman and of my appreciation for his remarkable vision of how the river in downtown San Antonio could -- and today, does -- look. While I never met Hugman himself, fortunately, I was able to meet Hugman's widow, Elene, his daughter, Anne -- Mrs. William Robinson -- and his son, Robert H.H. Hugman Jr. I also met Robert H. Turk, one of Hugman's closest friends and the superintendent of the WPA river development project during the late 1930's. I am deeply grateful to these people for providing me with valuable information and support while doing the research for this book.

Mr. and Mrs. Frank W. Phelps provided financial underwriting for the first edition. They were well-known for their interest in, and generosity toward, many River Walk projects. Mrs. Phelps died in 1991, and Mr. Phelps died in October of 1993. They will continue to be missed by their many friends along the San Antonio River Walk.

I am most grateful to the manuscript reviewers of the first edition: Lois Burkhalter, Dora Guerra, Rolly Hamilton and Ann Maria Watson.

The following individuals provided me with invaluable documents, information or suggestions for the first edition: Willie Alonzo, Daryl Engel, Jimmy Gause, Mary Grant, Franklin Hicks, Sandra Hood, Marianna Jones, Penn Jones, Ira Kennedy, Esther Macmillan, Elton Moy, Judy Robinson, Severo Rodriguez, Jessie Sanchez, Tom Shelton, David Straus, Irma Streng, Bernice Strong, Cy Wagner, Nelle Lee Weincek and Mary Ann Wimsatt.

Suggestions and information for the second edition came from the following: Keith Allen, U.S. Army Corps of Engineers; Diane Bruce, librarian, University of Texas at San Antonio Institute of Texan Cultures; Anne L. Cook, photo librarian, *Texas Highways* magazine, Texas Department of Transportation; Wayne Cox, archaeologist, the University of Texas at San Antonio; Ted Dracos, reporter for KENS-TV, and Robert Dunlop, former manager of Rivercenter mall;

Also: Dora Guerra, librarian for special collections at the University of Texas at San Antonio; Cindy Jimenez, staff of the Edwards Underground Water District; Patrick Kennedy, owner of La Mansion del Rio Hotel; Charles O. Kilpatrick, retired editor and publisher of the San Antonio Express-News; William Lyons, owner of Casa Rio Restaurant and Paseo del Rio Boats, Inc., and Russell Masters, former executive director of the Edwards Underground Water District;

Also: Patricia Osborne, retired City Historic Preservation Officer; Steven Ramsey, chief engineer of the San Antonio River Authority; Rosalind Rock, historian for the San Antonio Missions National Historical Park, and the staff of the Daughters of the Republic of Texas Library at the Alamo.

I am most grateful to La Mansion del Rio Hotel general manager Jan Leenders who encouraged me to write this revised edition and who suggested I use David Anthony Richelieu as editor. David also designed the new edition of the book. His suggestions have been invaluable throughout the process of putting the revision together.

His introduction to this edition is remarkably insightful. His words capture the flavor of the San Antonio River's history and the beauty and charm of the River Walk. The project also received extensive computer interface assistance from Claudette Mullen.

The revised edition includes virtually all the material from the first edition. New in this edition are an expanded history of the San Antonio River, facts about early San Antonio and its people and their ties to the river.

Also added is information about how the River Walk is managed, the latest flood control improvements to protect downtown and its River Walk, and outlines of recent long-range plans for future development of the entire river corridor.

Finally, I want to recognize the patience of my wife, Rosalie, who provided me with the support and encouragement needed to write this book. Without her inspiration and sense of humor, the entire project would have been less meaningful.

THE ARCHITECT

Robert H.H. Hugman

Robert Harvey Harold Hugman was born February 8, 1902, in San Antonio to Robert Charles Harold Hugman and Annie Weik Hugman, who lived on Westfall Street.

Following graduation from Brackenridge High School in February 1920, he entered the School of Architecture and Design at the University of Texas in Austin, which he attended from September 27, 1920, to June 5, 1924.

He married Martha Aurora Smith of Austin in June 1924 and shortly thereafter moved to New Orleans, Louisiana.

Their first child, Robert Harvey Harold Hugman, Jr. was born at the Touro Infirmary in New Orleans on March 8, 1925. A daughter, Anne Karin, was born 18 months later on October 15, 1926.

In the Spring of 1927, he and his family returned to San Antonio where he lived until his death on July 22, 1980, at the age of 78.

Photo from Elene Hugman

A BARGE CARRIES VISITORS PAST HISTORIC LANDMARKS LIKE THE TURRETED CLIFFORD BUILDING ON THE DOWNTOWN RIVER WALK, A SPECTACULAR LINEAR PARK DESIGNED BY ROBERT HUGMAN.
Texas Highways Magazine

INTRODUCTION

By David Anthony Richelieu

The logos or icons for the chapter headings are taken from the diverse patterns that Hugman created for the sidewalk panels along the River Walk.

The story of San Antonio is the story of its river.

The river is what has transformed the northern reaches of the great Mexican desert into a verdant oasis nestled against the stone escarpment where the land rises into the Texas Hill Country.

Small, meandering, unassuming, the San Antonio River is a sparkling ribbon of life.

During its most recent 300 years or so, the waters of the San Antonio River have shimmered with reflections of the people, places and events that are the historic legacy of the ninth largest city in the United States.

The river is the constant in the life of this city.

It gushes from the ground a few miles north of downtown from springs of a vast underground reservoir.

The Edwards Aquifer is enormous — 30 miles wide and 180 miles long and, some say, at least a mile deep.

The river's water nourishes banks whose lush greenery and towering trees have long been a refuge of shade and cool on the edge of an eternity of desolate, sun-bleached plains to the south and west.

The river is why usually nomadic Indian tribes had semi-permanent settlements at this place they called Yanaguana when history first noted the presence of European settlers here in 1691.

The river is why San Antonio is.

And why San Antonio is San Antonio.

In fact, when a Spanish expedition arrived June 13, 1691, on the feast day of St. Anthony of Padua, it was the river that was first named in his honor, then the place.

And the meandering river named for St. Anthony later gave life to five Spanish colonial missions that eventually grew into the City of San Antonio.

Built between 1718 and 1731, all five missions were established near the banks of the river so its clear, pure water could be diverted into a system of stone-lined channels, or acequias, leading into the mission compounds and to surrounding mission lands where crops and stock were raised.

The acequias were wonders of sophisticated gravity-flow engineering whose mechanical simplicity allowed them to remain in general use for nearly 200 years until a citywide underground water system was built early in the 20th Century.

Even more remarkably, some of the acequias remain in use today, still irrigating original mission farm lands.

And all five missions survive to this day, four as active Roman Catholic churches that are centerpieces of the San Antonio Missions National Historical Park.

The fifth mission, San Antonio de Valero, was the first to be established. That was in 1718. The mission was moved several times before its present siting atop a bank overlooking a sharp bend in the river.

It was on the banks of the San Antonio River near Mission Concepcion just south of the Alamo where, on October 28,

1835, a force under James Bowie won the first battle in the Texas war for independence.

It was on the banks of the river during the Battle of San Antonio in December of 1835 where Texas hero Ben Milam was shot in the head and killed by a sniper in a tree across the river when he stepped out the back door of the Veramendi House to relieve himself.

Then, in early 1836, the river became a blood-streaked witness to a 13-day siege and assault on Mission San Antonio, then known by its nickname, The Alamo.

What happened on the banks of the San Antonio River in 1836 became one of the most famous battles of all time and forever changed the course of history in the Western Hemisphere.

Mexico Gen. Antonio Lopez de Santa Anna had dismissed events at the Alamo as a small affair in his drive to quell rebellion among settlers and citizens in Texas.

Six weeks later, with "Remember the Alamo" as a battle cry, forces under Gen. Sam Houston defeated Santa Anna at San Jacinto near what is now the City of Houston.

That victory won independence from Mexico and created the Republic of Texas. And Texas stood as a separate, independent nation for nine years before joining the United States of America in 1845.

All that unfolded from an incident that took place on a bank of the San Antonio River where visitors today find a Hyatt Regency Hotel.

Actually, almost everything that happened along the San Antonio River can be blamed on the French.

If the French hadn't been in Louisiana and threatening the borders of New Spain, the viceroy in Mexico City might have never sent military and religious expeditions tramping through San Antonio to protect the border in East Texas.

The river might have not been named San Antonio, Mission San Antonio and the presidio never established, San Jose never founded and the three threatened missions in East Texas never moved here.

So, if it weren't for the French, there probably wouldn't be a city here today. Or a River Walk.

The river has been everything to San Antonio.

From earliest times, it has been the center of life in San Antonio. It was why people came here in 1691 and why people are still coming today.

The river has seen everything from baptisms to battles and from orangoutangs to grand opera along its banks.

The river and its bridges inspired poet Sidney Lanier and author William Porter, better known as O. Henry.

The river has been the city's drinking fountain, swimming pool, bathtub and toilet, the back door of businesses and the side door of river industries, such as the Daily Express, whose presses were powered by the river's flow, and the Dullnig Building, where river water became steam that powered the first commercial elevator in Texas. Today, that same building houses a McDonald's and a Taco Cabana Mexican restaurant, as well as the Taco Cabana corporate headquarters.

The river has been a source of fear and anger from repeated floods, especially in the early 1920's when downtown was under eight feet of water and 50 people lost their lives.

It was sometime after that disaster that Mayor Maury Maverick Sr., a bit wobbly and inebriated after a Democratic Party bash of some sort, was walking along with Police Commissioner Louis Lipscomb and stopped to relieve himself in the river, stumbled over some old tires and other debris, fell into the mud and water and declared then and there, "We've got to do something about this damned river."

The "something" eventually done by the city with the help of Maverick's friend Franklin D. Roosevelt and the Works Progress Administration was — well — really something. It is the San Antonio River Walk.

While the river coursing through downtown is so narrow that many call it a canal, it isn't. Its horseshoe bend with riverside development that attracts millions of people every year mostly follows the river's original natural route and still has a dirt bottom.

Remember, even the Mississippi begins modestly at Lake Itasca in northern Minnesota; so modestly one can cross it in two leaps using stepping stones. By the time it reaches the Twin Cities, the Mississippi is broad and mighty, flanked by towering smokestacks and huge grain elevators.

Not so, the San Antonio River.

Its business is beauty.

And its beauty has become big business.

Tourism in San Antonio is the city's No. 2 industry, right behind the city's five military bases.

Because of the genius and determination of young architect Robert H.H. Hugman, the river that was threatened in the 1920's with being filled in, paved over and made into a commercial street and drainage culvert, was transformed into a linear park of astonishing delight.

Its lush greenery and landscaping, trees, bridges, fountains, walks, stairs and benches create a serene setting one level beneath, but a world away from, downtown's hot, bustling streets. The stairs to the River Walk lead to an urban paradise where there are no traffic signals, growling vehicles or clouds of exhaust fumes.

The river begins in one of the city's largest parks and has many of San Antonio's great institutions and landmarks along its banks.

In Brackenridge Park, it passes through the San Antonio Zoo and provides water for the animals, wanders by the Witte Museum of Natural History and Science, then by the old Lone Star Brewery renovated into the San Antonio Museum of Art, curves behind the World War I memorial Municipal Auditorium and edges the Southwest Craft Center built in 1852 as the Ursuline Academy Catholic girls' school.

The river is the prized address of seven major hotels, a 21-story hospital and medical center, major financial institutions, three television stations and the city's original Carnegie Library that is now the Hertzberg Circus Museum.

On the river's banks are the city's tallest skyscrapers, two breweries, restaurants, night clubs, apartments, shops, townhouses, dining barges, live music, corporate headquarters, art galleries and an outdoor theater whose stage is on one side of the river and its terraced seating on the other.

When San Antonio threw a world's fair in 1968 to celebrate the 250th anniversary of the city's founding, the river was extended to a lagoon and stairway leading to the international exhibit area of HemisFair. Today, river barges drop guests and visitors off in the heart of the city's Convention Center that was built as part of the fair.

In 1988, the river extension acquired another branch leading into Rivercenter, a spectacular three-level shopping mall with towering glass walls that enclose the river basin.

This $250 million project includes more than 100 stores, two department stores, a 40-story Marriott Hotel, nine theaters, a comedy club, food court, several restaurants and an IMAX theater with a six-story screen where an IMAX movie about the Battle of the Alamo is shown several times a day.

Yes, many cities have built their downtowns on rivers that contributed significant chapters to their history.

But how many cities have rivers that attracted five Spanish colonial missions — missions that are still in existence? A dam, aqueduct and acequia system still working nearly 300 years later? The camp where Teddy Roosevelt trained recruits for his Rough Riders before charging up San Juan Hill?

How many rivers have banks where the Battle of the Alamo was fought?

San Antonio's tiny "canal" has constantly renewed and revived the city around it. Part of that is the river's natural beauty and human scale that invite contact and company. But the real renaissance of the river was a gift from a young architect who possessed an incredible future vision of what the San Antonio River should be.

It is on the River Walk where the river that meanders through the very center of the city, the storied history of San Antonio and the genius of Robert H.H. Hugman have evolved into a spectacular fusion of history, nature and circumstance.

For decades, San Antonio's missions were abandoned and in ruins. Restoration efforts began in the 1930's, and through the efforts of the Archdiocese of San Antonio, the Conservation Society and the State Parks and Wildlife Department, the four missions were repaired and restored as houses of worship and the Franciscan priests whose predecessors founded them were invited back.

By the late 1960's, the missions were acclaimed and recognized as the historic treasures they are . Efforts then began to create a national historical park embracing the missions.

About the same time work began to restore the missions, Robert Hugman was on a mission of his own. He not only joined the crusade to save the downtown river, but wanted to transform it into a romantic and historic experience that would be a natural asset and — as he predicted over and over again in the late 1920's and through the 1930's — would also spur business activity and growth.

Surely, fate had a hand in the ironic twist of Hugman's river plan being approved by a special city committee, only to be rejected by the mayor and the City Commission who promised no new spending because of the Depression. Then, in 1939, the recovery plan launched to end the Depression provided the funds needed to build the River Walk.

Just as incredible was that after its completion, Hugman's River Walk just sat there — ignored, unused and even dubbed as "dangerous" — for more than 20 years.

A building boom in the late 1920s included the Aztec, Texas and Majestic theaters, Municipal Auditorium, the Smith-Young Tower (now, the Tower Life Building), the Milam Building, Express-News Building, Alamo National Bank Building, the Plaza Hotel (now the Granada Apartments), Nix Hospital, the Casino Club, the Medical Arts Building (now the Emily Morgan Hotel), the Federal Reserve Bank (now the Consulate General of Mexico), the Main Library (now the Hertzberg Circus Museum), the Scottish Rite Cathedral and the Southwestern Bell Telephone Building on Auditorium Circle.

But the Depression lingered in San Antonio forever and downtown seemed frozen in time for at least three decades. The new U.S. Court House and Post Office on Alamo Plaza (1937) and the Alameda Theater (1949) were the only major additions to downtown until the new 18-story headquarters for the National Bank of Commerce was built in 1957.

When the stock market crashed, San Antonio was the largest city in Texas. Many still blame the city's failure to build facilities to house the Texas State Fair for San Antonio's subsequent decades of decline when it was eclipsed in size and prominence, first, by Dallas — which welcomed the state fair with open arms — and then by Houston.

Finally, the plague of suburban sprawl that was killing big-city downtowns all across America in the 1960's spread to San Antonio. Merchants fled in droves from Houston Street, the city's former retail shopping stem, in a rush to new malls out in "Loopland," as the area along Loop 410 is called. Downtown was wheezing and gasping and teetering near the grave.

City leaders decided a world's fair might help, and spent years planning and politicking and pushing HemisFair '68 to reality.

Only seven million of the predicted 10 million visitors came to the fair. Its many attractions included two open-air IBM pavilions where fair-goers could sit and play with new-fangled TV-looking gadgets called computer terminals and could talk by PicturePhone to folks at a Bell Telephone exhibit in Chicago — just like the call made on movie screens that year from a space station to earth in Stanley Kubrick's epic: "2001: A Space Odyssey."

HemisFair's 92 acres delighted everyone who came, including national news magazines, who dubbed it a "jewel-box of a fair." HemisFair also brought the city its first major new hotel (the Palacio del Rio) in years and saw the first new cluster of shops and restaurants open on the long-ignored River Walk.

Suddenly, the world was raving about downtown's masterpiece on the river that Hugman had designed four decades earlier. And the city itself suddenly rediscovered its River Walk that was just sitting there waiting to happen.

As downtown street shopping withered, the River Walk was alive with music, celebrations, new restaurants, shops and a rush of new hotel construction.

Surveys started listing San Antonio as the favorite tourist destination in Texas, as well as the favorite escape for folks so busy making it in the "super city" boomtowns of Dallas and Houston.

San Antonio mistakenly began dynamiting its old buildings and creating barren plains of parking lots in an attempt to copy the urban thinking of Dallas and Houston.

But people kept saying the reason they liked coming to San Antonio was because of its atmosphere and old buildings and especially because "it doesn't look like Dallas or Houston."

In the early '70's, San Antonio wrote and passed the first historic preservation ordinance in Texas and opened its City Historic Preservation Office. By 1988, the city had inventoried and protected 1,100 downtown buildings as officially designated city historic landmarks, plus those in 10 geographically defined historic districts around the city.

History became the city's treasured currency in the exploding billion-dollar tourism market. And there sat Hugman's River Walk, so deliberately and purposely designed with romantic Old World architecture reflecting the historic legacy of the most historic city in Texas.

The hotel boom continued along the River Walk and, in 1988, the 40-story, 1,000 room Marriott opened in Rivercenter, the spectacular three-story mall built right behind the Alamo and clustered around a new River Walk lagoon on the river extension.

Because of Hugman's River Walk, when downtowns across the country were fading fast in urban renewal intensive care wards, San Antonio opened Rivercenter and downtown saw 120 new stores open all at once on the same day.

Rivercenter revived downtown shopping. Meanwhile, several other new hotels had opened and restaurants and shops all along the River Walk began expanding to accommodate the growing crowds of conventioneers and visitors from other Texas cities who had fallen in love with downtown San Antonio.

While downtown hotels in other cities offered weekend specials trying to fill some of their empty rooms until regular business travelers returned on Mondays, hotels in downtown San Antonio started putting up "No Vacancy" signs weekend after weekend.

Downtown San Antonio, in fact, thrived right through the collapse of the Texas oilpatch and real estate market in the late '80's that triggered failures of most of the state's banks and savings and loans.

Today, downtown San Antonio is alive with people and excitement at night, and especially on weekends. That makes it the envy of other downtowns — including Dallas and Houston — that on most nights and weekends are like ghost towns of empty office towers.

It was almost miraculous, but certainly no coincidence, that Hugman recognized the importance of showcasing history in his design of the River Walk and that, decades later, the city suddenly discovered history was the dynamo of its growing $2 billion per year tourism industry.

The city is capitalizing on history because its charm was recognized and emphasized by Robert Hugman 60 years ago in his fascinating and wonderfully detailed visions for developing something he called the River Walk.

Hugman achieved historic ambience along the River Walk through a masterful combination of formal design and natural ease. His bridges and stairwell walls and finials with shapes in grand flourishes of the baroque are tempered by the natural, rough-finish stone and other native materials that create an exquisitely balanced sense of casual elegance.

The success of Hugman's River Walk was because the comprehensive vision set down in his architectural plans extended to even the smallest of details — a fact he underscored by insisting that the dream could be realized only if taken as a whole.

Indeed, his basic Spanish style plan was embellished by details in a variety of different designs that provide many changing experiences and moods along the river. That diversity is such a marvelous unity precisely because all the diverse but complementary parts came in a single visionary flash from the mind of one person.

In 1988, when the city attempted to bring the ambience of the River Walk up to street-level with the TriParty Project, more than two dozen architects and architectural firms from San Antonio and Dallas struggled mightily to create this same sort of unity from diversity. Instead, the $42 million project resulted in an often-embarrassing Babylon of many design ideas and motifs.

One can only imagine how the River Walk might look today if, instead of reflecting Hugman's singular vision, it had been created by committee.

But it wasn't. And Hugman's genius in detailing a total plan for the River Walk was recognized in the 1980's when a national committee of the American Institute of Architects acclaimed Hugman's River Walk as America's finest example of urban design.

This book then pays tribute to those from the Spanish explorers and missionaries to River Walk architect Robert H.H. Hugman and those today who continue his vision of seeing the San Antonio River for what it is — the center of everything in San Antonio.

It is officially the second most-popular visitor attraction in Texas, behind only the Alamo. But there isn't a truly accurate count of all who enjoy the River Walk every day.

Some insist that the River Walk attracts far more people than the Alamo. Whatever the case, having the Alamo and the River Walk right across the street from each other in the middle of downtown makes San Antonio the envy of cities everywhere.

The river, simply put, is just an incredible experience.

Enjoying chipotle-spiced Mexican beef tips on the balcony of a riverside restaurant while watching people stroll along or glide by in barges that pass under gracefully arched bridges above the sparkling water and all under a breathtaking canopy of towering trees is a simple joy that can't be experienced just anywhere. In fact, almost nowhere else.

Perhaps San Antonians take the river and its River Walk for granted these days. But visitors love our downtown as "the most European" of America's cities and guests from Mexico exclaim how much they feel at home.

We sometimes seem embarrassed by our riches and for having ignored the river, and for literally turning our backs — and our buildings' backs — on it for decades.

The story of how the River Walk was envisioned and built has surprises much like those found along the River Walk itself when being discovered for the first time by a visitor or a newcomer to San Antonio.

Some may discover the River Walk for the first time on the pages of this book. If that is the case, enjoy your casual stroll along this delightful, meandering stream of San Antonio history. Like San Antonio itself, the River Walk is an original. And a real piece of work.

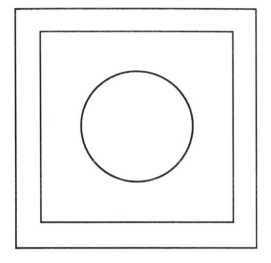

CHAPTER ONE

A Historical Glimpse Of the River

The San Antonio River's colorful written history begins with its discovery by Spanish military and religious expeditions that claimed the river and its environs in the name of the crown. Because of the abundance and quality of the water flowing from the springs that feed it, the small, winding stream was a magnet that drew early settlers to its lush, shaded banks.

Now, 300 years later, it remains a magnet that attracts millions of people from around the world who also flock to its banks to drink in its charm, beauty and atmosphere. As we reflect on the history of San Antonio and its river, we must recognize the importance of assuring that this natural treasure maintain its significant past into the 21st Century.

The San Antonio River's headwaters once flowed freely from springs bubbling out of limestone crevices in an area that is now a part of the campus of Incarnate Word College. The college's yearbooks up to and including the 1940's recalled boating, hiking and horseback-riding along the banks of the river and in its creeks and ponds.

However, in the 1950's, a severe drought saw the spring flow cease. In the early 1970's, the college cleared the area for playing fields, but when heavy rains returned, the new fields were turned into water gardens as the headwaters resumed their natural flow.

As Dick McCracken, the college's informal historian, put it, "the next two decades kept campus leaders guessing to whether the river was somnambulant or comatose."

In the 1990's, the San Antonio River continues to be reborn during periods of heavy rainfall. For example, in the spring of 1992, a baseball game at Incarnate Word College had to be canceled due to wet grounds from the spring flow. Indeed, the headwaters of the San Antonio River are quite like the proverbial sleeping giant that sometimes is docile and quiet, while at other times reveals incredible energy.[1]

While San Antonio River springs flow freely after long periods of heavy rains, the volume of water isn't always sufficient to maintain water needed downstream for the River Walk. To maintain proper water levels in the downtown river area, the city installed large pumps near the natural headwaters. The wells pump approximately 5 million gallons of water a day into the river when there is no spring flow.[2]

During severe dry spells, up to 11 million gallons a day are pumped to keep the downtown river area full of water.

Recently, under the direction of the U.S. Army Corps of Engineers, two large flood bypass tunnels were excavated under downtown to handle massive flood runoff.

These same tunnels can also recycle water in that stretch of the river and will be able to maintain an acceptable depth and flow with only a minimum of fresh water added to the river.

PATH OF THE RIVER

From its headwaters, the river winds through downtown San Antonio. To cover six linear miles, the river meanders 15 miles through the heart of the city, passing historical landmarks, skyscrapers and the sites of epic events.

From San Antonio, the river heads south through six counties: Bexar, Wilson, Karnes, Goliad, Refugio, and Victoria. It passes near the towns of Floresville, Karnes City, and Goliad before emptying into the Guadalupe River a few miles inland from San Antonio Bay on the Gulf of Mexico.

A map on Page 20 shows the path of the San Antonio River from its headwaters north of downtown San Antonio to its mouth.

The river is augmented by several tributaries en route, including the Medina River. Olmos Creek joins the river near its headwaters while Alazan, Salado and San Pedro creeks merge with it at different points in San Antonio and Bexar County. In Karnes County, the Escondido and Ecleto creeks flow into the river and in Goliad County, the Hord and Manahuilla creeks join it.[3]

THE EDWARDS AQUIFER

The spring flow during heavy rainy seasons is actually a "discharge" from the Edwards Aquifer, which is often referred to as a "Texas Treasure," not of gold or silver, but a cache of crystal pure water.

The discharge from the aquifer occurs naturally when the water level reaches approximately 665 feet above sea level at the San Antonio Springs in Brackenridge Park. The San Pedro Springs begin flowing when water in the aquifer reaches 660 feet above sea level.

The Edwards Aquifer began forming about 100 million years ago when Texas as we know it was part of a shallow sea. As the inland seas receded, layers of shell and coral were deposited. These layers turned into porous honeycombed limestone rock which formed the Edwards Aquifer.

Today, the aquifer is the principal source of water for some 1.3 million people and has supported human habitation for over 8,000 years. This aquifer is one of the nation's most remarkable, extending 180 miles from Brackettville in Kinney County south of San Antonio to Kyle in Hays County north of San Antonio near Austin. The recharge zone, encompassing 1,500 square miles, is known as the Balcones Fault Zone. See the drawing and map on the facing page.

The Texas Hill Country is the drainage area known as the Edwards Plateau and captures much of the water that runs down and soaks into the aquifer's underground limestone. This area covers approximately 4,400 square miles. The recharge zone provides a pathway of fractures, sinkholes and caves for the water to reach the artesian area. About 70 per cent of the total recharge comes from Uvalde and Kinney counties.

The Artesian/Reservoir area underlies six counties: Kinney, Uvalde, Medina, Bexar, Comal, and Hays. Along its 180-mile length, the aquifer varies from 5 to 30 miles in width. The reservoir area covers an estimated 2,100 square miles.

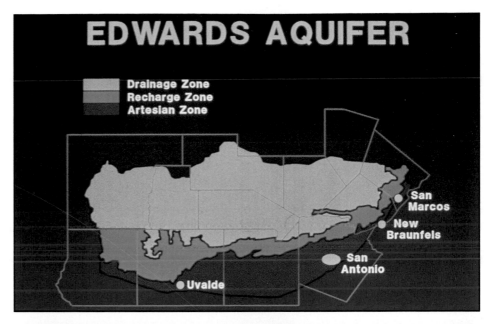

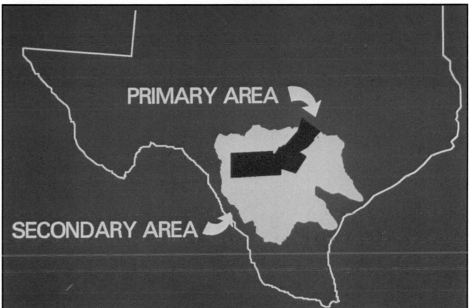

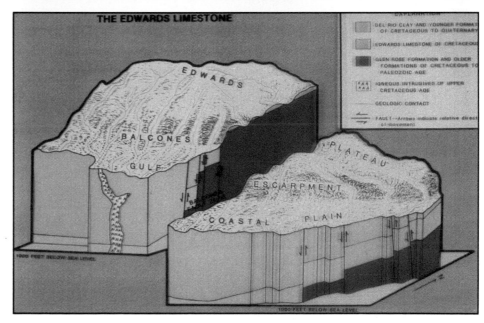

Maps and Diagrams from the Edwards Underground Water District

RARE INTERIOR PHOTO OF THE ALAMO, SHRINE OF TEXAS LIBERTY, SHOWS THE SIX FLAGS OVER TEXAS AND DISPLAY CASES.
Texas Highways Magazine

In 1940, the aquifer region was pumping 120,100 acre-feet annually, an amount equivalent to about 39 billion gallons. In the 1990's, pumping reached 542,000 acre-feet, or over 176 billion gallons. By the year 2020, annual demand could reach 850,000 acre-feet. Since annual recharge of the aquifer averages only 640,000 acre-feet, water conservation is obviously necessary. Plans are now under way to construct dams that can capture additional runoff and conservation will likely become mandatory throughout the entire aquifer region.

In 1959, the Texas Legislature created the Edwards Underground Water District to monitor and protect this natural resource. In 1989, rural counties west of San Antonio withdrew from the Edwards district, shattering attempts by San Antonio Mayor Henry Cisneros to forge a regional consensus to manage usage of the aquifer.

In 1992, the Texas Water Commission attempted to effect regional controls over the Edwards by declaring it an underground river, thus making it subject to the state's comprehensive surface water regulations.

But farmers and others insisted on maintaining their rights under a turn-of-the-century court ruling granting property owners full ownership and unlimited use of all water "under their land."

Despite the obvious scientific error of Texas water law that refuses to recognize that with an aquifer, the water under one person's land is the same water that is under everyone else's land, farmers from Uvalde County and others went into state district court and successfully stymied the state's attempt to manage the aquifer by limiting the amount of water various categories of users could pump from the Edwards, depending on its water level.

Meanwhile, a trial was held in federal court on a suit filed by the Sierra Club and others charging the U.S. Department of Interior with failing to enforce the Endangered Species Act in protecting small aquatic species at the aquifer's Comal Springs at New Braunfels and the San Marcos Springs in San Marcos.

After lengthy arguments before U.S. District Judge Lucius Bunton in Midland, the state was given until the summer of 1993 to prepare a comprehensive and workable plan for management of the Edwards Aquifer that would meet standards set by the U.S. Fish and Wildlife Service for protecting the endangered species.

In May of 1993, the Texas Legislature adopted a plan similar to the water commission plan rejected by state courts and created an appointive agency, the Edwards Aquifer Authority, to "manage, protect, and conserve the aquifer."[4]

As of this printing, the new aquifer management plan and state-established aquifer authority were being challenged before the U.S. Justice Department to determine whether the appointed board replacing the Edwards Underground Water District's elected board complied with the Voting Rights Act.

THE LUSH GREENERY AND ABUNDANT WATER OF THE SAN ANTONIO RIVER HAVE ATTRACTED PEOPLE TO ITS BANKS FOR AT LEAST 10,000 YEARS. IT WAS AN OASIS FOR BOTH NATIVE INDIANS AND SPANISH MILITARY AND MISSIONARY EXPEDITIONS.
The Institute of Texan Cultures

If cleared by the Justice Department, the plan then would face a complete review by Judge Bunton before implementation.

EARLY HISTORY

There is good evidence from the discoveries of archaeologists to suggest that humans lived near the San Antonio River more than 10,000 years ago. Traces of human habitation in and around the Olmos Basin, and near the headwaters of the San Antonio River, were discovered by David Orchard during construction of the Olmos Dam in the 1920's. His personal collection of flint projectile points and pottery shards were characteristic of an earlier and primitive time.[5]

Archaeologist Wayne Cox, who has explored several areas near the San Antonio River, explained that flood waters over the centuries washed away most traces of very early human habitation. However, he agrees that humans did, indeed, live near and around the San Antonio River for over 10,000 years before recorded history by Spanish and French explorers noted the discovery of Indians living near the river's waters.

It is now known that in 1535, Alvar Nunez Cabeza de Vaca crossed the San Antonio River during explorations inland from the Gulf of Mexico.

According to Thomas L. Hester, the Payaya Indians were a hunting and gathering nomadic peoples and when the Spaniards arrived in the area now known as San Antonio, they observed Payaya settlements near streams, particularly by the San Antonio River and San Pedro Springs.

Because the Payaya frequently moved and occupied different encampments, it may have led to the confusion evident in diaries from early Spanish expeditions over whether the Payaya lived by the San Antonio River or San Pedro Springs. It is likely they lived at both places at various times. Other Indian tribes also lived in and around San Antonio, depending on available food and the season of the year.[6]

Two of the earliest descriptions of the San Antonio River were written in 1691 during an expedition led by Gov. Domingo Teran de los Rios, whose entourage included ecclesiastical aide, Father Damian Massanet.

They reached the environs of San Antonio on June 12, and moved north the next day.

Gov. Teran's diary notes the expedition's arrival in the area included seeing great numbers of buffalo, then adds:

> "On the 13th, our royal standard and camp proceeded in the same easterly direction. We traveled five leagues (approximately 13 miles) over fine country — broad plains, the most beautiful in New Spain. We camped on the banks of a stream adorned by a great stand of trees . . . . I named it San Antonio de Padua because we reached it on his day. Here we

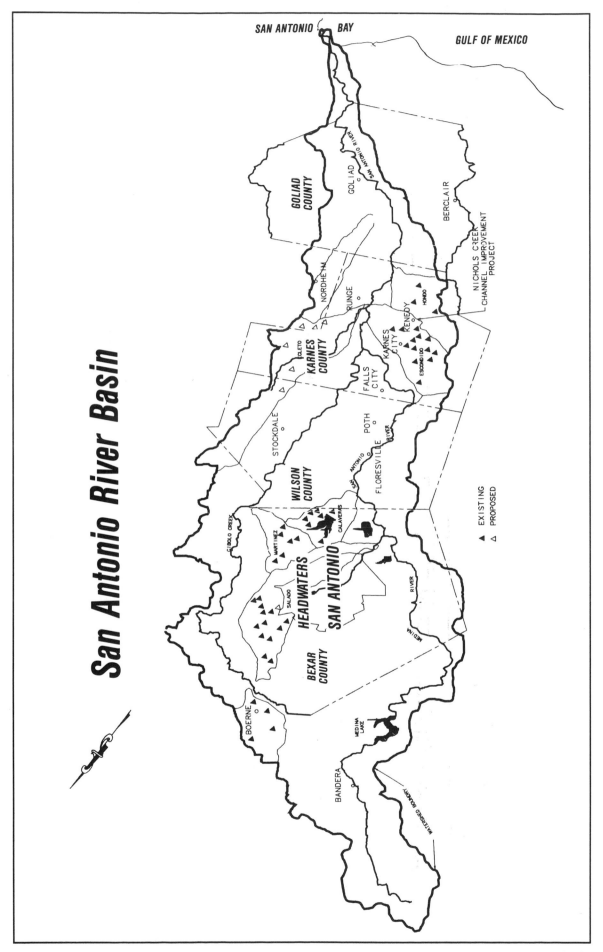

San Antonio River Basin

San Antonio River Authority

found an encampment of the Payaya tribe. We observed their actions and I concluded that they were docile and affectionate, naturally friendly and very well disposed toward us. I saw the opportunity of using them to form missions."

In his diary entry for June 13, Massanet wrote:

"We continued northeast, a quarter east, until we passed through some low hills covered with oaks and mesquites. The country is very beautiful. We entered a stretch which was easy for travel and advanced on our easterly course. Before reaching the river, there are other small hills with large oaks. The river is bordered with many trees, cottonwoods, oaks, cedars, mulberries, and many vines. There are a great many fish, and upon the highlands a great number of wild chickens.

"On this day, there were so many buffaloes that the horses stampeded and 40 head ran away . . . . I called this place San Antonio de Padua, because it was his day. In the language of the Indians, it is called Yanaguana.", [7]

According to accounts of the Espinosa-Olivares-Aguirre Expedition of 1709 by noted church historian Carlos E. Castaneda, the river was named for San Antonio de Padua on April 8, 1709, by Franciscan priests, Antonio de San Buenaventura Olivares and Isidro de Espinosa.

At the same time, they named a major spring that flows into the San Antonio River as San Pedro Springs. Espinosa's diary, as translated by Gabriel Tous, included this description:

"At a short distance, we came to a luxuriant growth of trees, high walnuts, poplars, elms and mulberries watered by a copious spring which rises near a populous rancheria of Indians of the tribes Siupan, Chaulames and some of the Sijames, numbering in all about 500 persons, young and old.

"The river, which is formed by this spring, could supply not only a village, but a city which could easily be founded here because of the good ground and the many conveniences, and because of the shallowness of said river. This river, not having been named by the Spaniards, we called it the River of San Antonio de Padua." [8]

The conflicting information about who named the San Antonio River has been debated by historians, but both times the

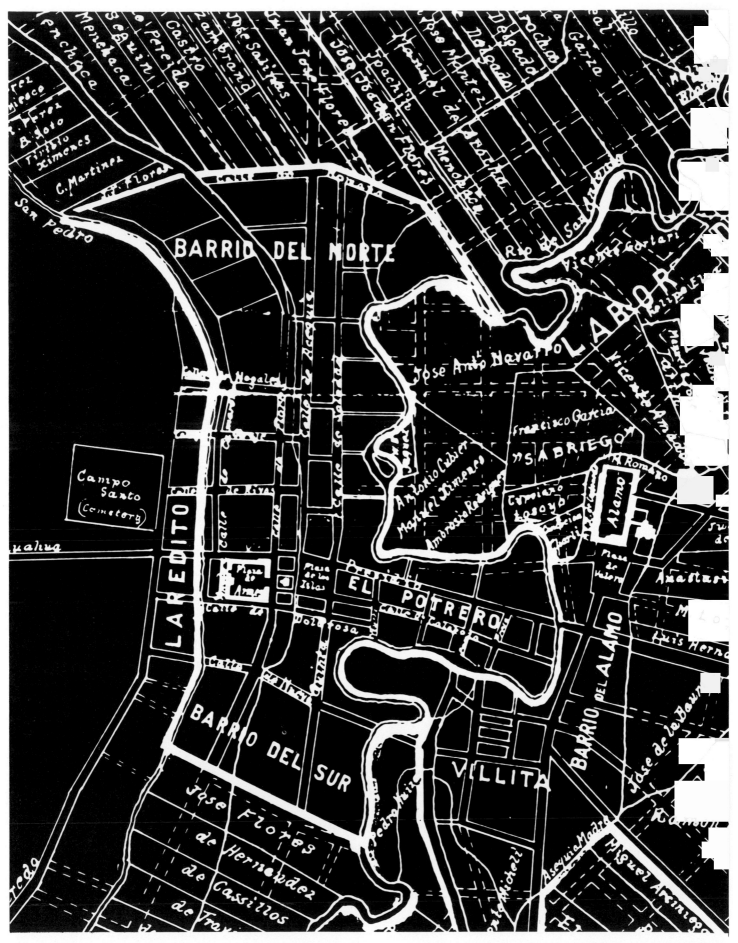

MAP OF LANDS GIVEN TO CANARY ISLAND SETTLERS USED THE SAN ANTONIO RIVER AND SAN PEDRO CREEK AS CITY BOUNDARIES.
The University of Texas at San Antonio Special Collections

river was named in honor of St. Anthony of Padua, a Franciscan priest who was born in Lisbon, Portugal, August 5, 1195. He was ordained in 1220 and was famed as a teacher and scholar in Italy and his native Portugal. He died at age 36 in Padua, Italy, June 13, 1231, and was later proclaimed Portugal's national saint.

The naming controversy poses some intriguing possibilities. Logic supports the 1691 diaries because the arrival date and naming correspond to the feast of St. Anthony, which was mentioned in both diaries as the reason for choosing that name.

The 1709 expedition arrived on April 8, the feast of Walter of Pontoise. If Olivares followed the well-established tradition of honoring the saint on whose day great events occur, he should have named it the Walter River.

One historian suggests it may be more than mere coincidence that Father Olivares' name was Antonio and Captain Aquirre, the group's military escort, was named Pedro. Antonio, San Antonio River. Pedro, San Pedro Creek.

Most dismiss the river naming and simply credit the 1709 expedition with locating and naming San Pedro Creek.

At a Mass on the San Antonio River the evening of June 13, 1969, as San Antonians observed the feast day of St. Anthony, the City of San Antonio formally dedicated an eight-foot bronze statue of St. Anthony that was a gift from Portugal on the occasion of HemisFair '68, the world's fair celebrating the 250th anniversary of the city's founding.

The statue had been in front of the Portuguese Pavilion during HemisFair and now stands on the north bank of the river near the turn into Rivercenter mall.[9]

The French presence in Louisiana had prompted the Spanish presence in San Antonio. The race to claim land we now know of as Texas was strongly contested by Spain and France in the early 1700's. Those hostilities caused Spain's viceroy in Mexico City to develop missions, villas and presidios along the San Antonio River.

On April 9, 1718, 72 persons left Coahuila for San Antonio de Padua with cattle, sheep, goats, chickens and horses. They arrived April 25th and were joined by Father Antonio Olivares on May 1st.

Mission San Antonio de Valero (later known as the Alamo) was established by the leader of the expedition, new Texas Gov. Martin de Alarcon, at a site generally believed to be on the west side of the San Antonio River near San Pedro Springs. The exact location remains unknown.

May 5 saw the founding of the Villa de Bejar, pronounced Bay-har. In Mexican Spanish that reflects the influence of the Aztec language, an Indian X often is used in place of the Spanish J, but both are pronounced the same way.

In January of 1722, a presidio (military garrison) was erected on a site now called Military Plaza but then known as Plaza de Armas. The garrison became known as San Antonio de Bejar.[10]

The suffixes of the names of the mission (de Valero) and the villa (de Bejar) honored Don Baltazar de Zuniga, Marques de Valero, who was the Viceroy of New Spain in Mexico City, and financed the expedition to San Antonio. The Bejar name honors the Duke de Bejar, the viceroy's brother, who died a national hero of Spain while defending Budapest against the invading Turks.

After news of fertile lands, abundant water and timber and the possibility of mining precious metals in Texas reached the Spanish Court of King Phillip V, His Majesty issued several royal decrees intended to encourage Spanish families from the Canary Islands to settle in New Spain, particularly in Texas.

It was originally intended that some of the colonists establish a villa on Espiritu Santo Bay (now Matagorda Bay) to help protect the coastline from further encroachments by the French in neighboring Louisiana. After stops in Havana and Veracruz, the Canary Islanders learned the colonization plan had been canceled because Mission San Antonio and its presidio that were founded in 1718, were thriving well enough as the beginnings of a permanent villa, so there was no longer a need for additional settlers.

Still, the group headed overland and 56 of them reached San Antonio on March 9, 1731.

They named their settlement Villa de San Fernando in honor of the king's son and heir to the Spanish throne. This Spanish colonial town, Villa de San Fernando, was surveyed and laid out according to a standard plan set forth in the Laws of the Indies, published circa 1681. On July 2, 1731, each family collected large stones and stakes as markers for the land they were to receive.

The site of the church was crucial, since it was to be the starting point for laying out the land. The Church of San Fernando, now a cathedral, is the geographical axis of the city. The division of the city's streets by north, south, east and west begins at the front doors of the church on what is now called Main Plaza.

San Fernando is one of the most historic churches in the country. The Spanish colonial stone and adobe domed church completed in 1749 remains intact at the rear of the 19th Century French Gothic front expansion begun in 1868 by Francois Giraud.

An architect who served two terms as mayor of San Antonio, Giraud also designed part of the Ursuline Academy, now the Southwest Craft Center where a private club is named in his honor. Giraud also did the survey for Mayor Sam Maverick defining the original boundaries of the walls, buildings and other structures of the Alamo compound that were destroyed during and after the Battle of the Alamo.

San Fernando, the oldest cathedral in the United States, is where Alamo hero Jim Bowie married Ursula Veramendi, daughter of the vice governor. The church was used as a look-

THE HISTORIC SAN FERNANDO CATHEDRAL.
Convention and Visitors Bureau

out by Santa Anna's forces, who camped around it during the Battle of the Alamo.

It was from San Fernando's steeple (removed later when the twin-towered gothic front was added) that Santa Anna flew the "No Quarter" flag to signal the Alamo defenders he would take no prisoners and show no mercy.

The settlers of Villa de San Fernando established the first civilian government in all of Texas, one of the tasks assigned in the royal decree ordering their journey to San Antonio.

Again, the river played a key role in the life of San Antonio.

When the Canary Islanders attempted to layout the villa using the standard city plan from the Law of the Indies, the location of the river and the slope of the land required that the plan be flipped in reverse.

That relocated several buildings surrounding Plaza Mayor, or Main Plaza, including San Fernando Church. The flipped plan is why San Fernando faces east instead of west in the long-established tradition of Catholic Churches throughout the world.

Eventually, the irrigable farm plots (known as long lots) were designated in length by the distance from San Pedro Creek to the San Antonio River. These lots were about 290 feet wide and from 1,300 to 5,000 feet in length. They were choice lots because of the availability of water. [11]

From 1718 to 1731, San Antonio was variously known as San Antonio de Padua, Villa de Bejar, Villa de San Fernando de Bexar and San Antonio de Bexar. The city has kept its original name and the county name now honors the Duke of Bexar.

Sources of water had been carefully recorded in logs of expeditions to Texas by the French and Spanish as early as the 15th and 16th centuries. But when the Europeans arrived as settlers, the struggle to gain control of water resources began in earnest.

Spain avoided major controversy among its settlers by developing a clever plan to distribute water by building canals and waterways called acequias. These water courses were an integral part of life in early San Antonio. They were constructed to furnish fresh water to the villa and missions and provide irrigation for farm lands. In most places, the channels were ditches carved into the ground, often lined with rock and mortar. Occasionally, they included above-ground aqueducts. [12]

The acequias were vital to the development of the missions in San Antonio.

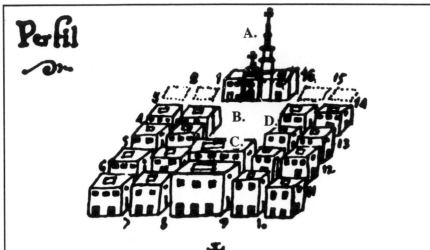

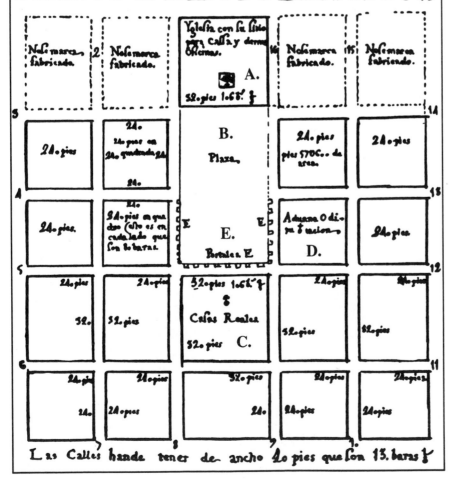

PLANO DE LA POBLACION.

Villa de San Fernando de Bexar

These original maps of San Fernando de Bexar were prepared for the settlers from the Canary Islands who arrived here in 1731. The plans were based on the Laws of the Indies that established uniform standards for cities in New Spain.

This translation by Louis Viramontes is from maps filed in the General and Public Archives in Mexico City. Copies were obtained from the Institute of Texan Cultures.

This plan and drawing look west to east, showing San Fernando Church on the east side of the plaza

The slope of the land, and its proximity to the river, persuaded the settlers to flip the plan and place the church on the west side of the plaza away from the river. That caused the church to be built facing east, instead of west, the traditional direction for Catholic churches.

Profile

In this manner, and with this facade, the town that is shown in this plan and described below will be established. The letters and numbers correspond to the site where they are located, conforming one to the other.
Established Construction.

PLAN OF THE CITY

A. Church with its location for house and other offices. 100 varas or 320 feet wide.

The blocks at the top with dotted lines are marked, "No se marca fabricado," which means "No construction noted."

B. Plaza.
C. Governor's Palace.
D. Customs or deputation.
E. Portals to the Plaza.

The streets shall be 40 feet wide, the equivalent of 13 varas.

The standard square blocks flanking the plaza are 240 feet or 80 varas per side, covering a total of 57,600 square feet.

CHAPTER TWO

The River and The Missions

Like dozens of Indian tribes before them, the Spaniards were drawn to San Antonio by its river and its abundant water. The river is the reason why expeditions from two colleges of Franciscan missionaries in New Spain -- at Queretaro and Zacatecas -- were sent to San Antonio and why, along a 10-mile stretch of its banks, they established five missions between 1718 and 1731.

The missions of San Antonio are remarkable for several reasons. The architecture of Mission San Antonio de Valero and Mission San Jose, for example, are almost inexplicably ornate and elaborate celebrations of Spanish baroque elegance amid harsh, isolated and hostile surroundings.

Unlike many mission churches of Arizona and other parts of the Southwest, the missions of San Antonio were not made of adobe or clay blocks covered with stucco. The missions of San Antonio were constructed of large limestone blocks quarried in the area and moved to the site.

One can only guess the reaction of curious natives in the area as the missionaries taught those who were interested the remarkable skills that enabled them to build structures more magnificent than anything they had ever seen or imagined.

The Spaniards gave special meaning to the notion of the Church Triumphant.

It is clear that even here, along the desolate, primitive northern frontiers of New Spain, souls would be won in impressive buildings that were designed to overwhelm and awe.

These were no humble, unassuming chapels. Despite total isolation from cities with skilled craftsmen and artisans, the Franciscan missionaries somehow, in the middle of nowhere, knew enough advanced building skills to be able to teach the nomadic Indians skills and knowledge of materials.

The Indians would be helped by craftsmen brought in from time to time. Together, they built splendid church buildings with doorways and facades that today are recognized as masterpieces of the stonecutter's art.

The fronts of Mission San Antonio and Mission San Jose were adorned with twisted baroque columns, fanciful ornamentation of glorious complexity, niches with conch framing, expressive statues of the saints and the Virgin of Guadalupe.

The stucco-covered interior and exterior walls were accented with vivid decorative patterns done in stains and paints made from the muds, red clays and other natural pigments in the area.

As astounding as the artistry and architecture of the missions were the acequias, marvels of engineering and hydrological science that brought the fresh, abundant waters of the San Antonio River to the missions and their grounds.

Built as part of each mission was a small dam and a network of stone-lined channels called acequias that let gravity

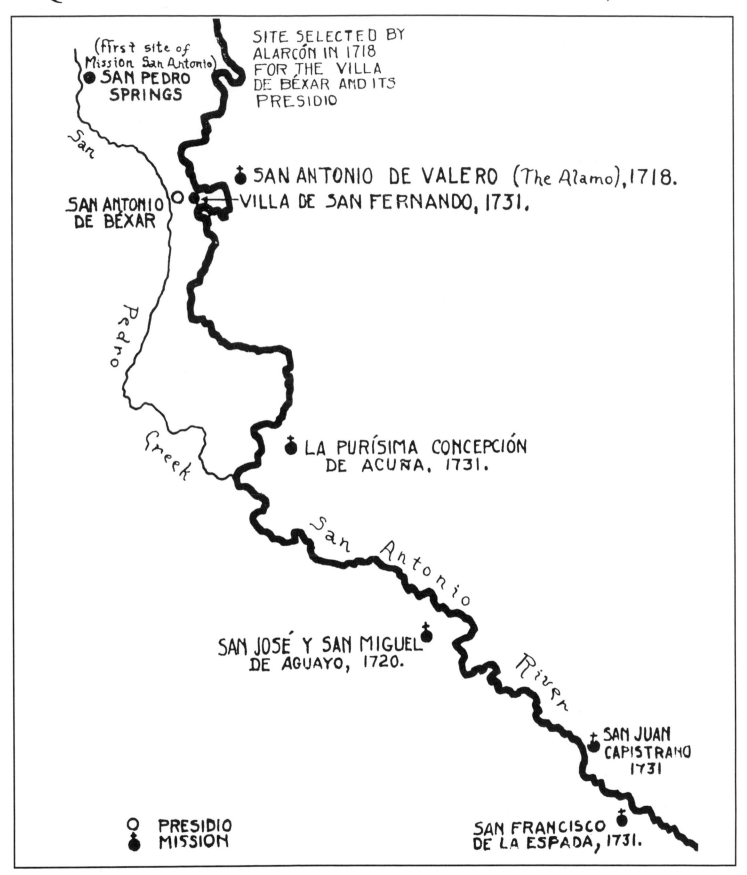

(First site of Mission San Antonio)
SAN PEDRO SPRINGS

SITE SELECTED BY ALARCÓN IN 1718 FOR THE VILLA DE BÉXAR AND ITS PRESIDIO

SAN ANTONIO DE VALERO (The Alamo), 1718.

VILLA DE SAN FERNANDO, 1731.

SAN ANTONIO DE BÉXAR

San Pedro Creek

LA PURÍSIMA CONCEPCIÓN DE ACUÑA, 1731.

San Antonio River

SAN JOSÉ Y SAN MIGUEL DE AGUAYO, 1720.

SAN JUAN CAPISTRANO 1731

PRESIDIO
MISSION

SAN FRANCISCO DE LA ESPADA, 1731.

SAN ANTONIO, 1718-1731

carry the river water to the compound where it was used for drinking, bathing, livestock and crop irrigation.

These, too, were constructed by Indian converts under the supervision of the missionary priests.

Because of the river, San Antonio was chosen as the site for five missions.

And, because of their stone walls, the successful construction of miles of acequias, and fortunate circumstance, these outposts of Spanish civilization flourished decades longer than anyone ever intended.

Even more remarkable, despite periods of neglect, all five missions are in use today. The Alamo is a state-owned shrine and museum. The other four missions remain as active parish churches and also are part of the San Antonio Missions National Historical Park.

San Antonio is the only city with five Spanish colonial missions.

San Antonio has the only functioning Spanish colonial water distribution system in the nation. And the water system still irrigates farms that were part of the original mission lands.

And some of those lands today belong to direct descendants of farmers who once lived at the missions and later inherited pieces of original mission lands. That occurred when the Franciscans withdrew at the end of the 18th Century and turned the mission churches over to the local parish priests in what was then the largest city in Texas.

The place of the missions in San Antonio has often been misunderstood, and some have mistakenly declared them failures.

Each mission was intended to be a small city where native families were invited to move inside and live in apartments or quarters in the perimeter walls.

Between classes on religion, the mission residents learned to farm, raise cattle and other livestock, irrigate, weave, read and write — and build.

The mission compounds were designed to protect the inhabitants from attacks by hostiles and renegades.

Presidios housing garrisons of Spanish soldiers also were built near missions to assure protection both for those living in the compound and while working the mission's surrounding crop and grazing lands.

The establishment of the missions in Texas required one major ingredient — an abundance of water. The San Antonio River more than met that requirement.

The Spaniards realized the missions must be self-sustaining. Without ample fresh water, this goal was unattainable.

The primary purpose of the missions was to convert Indians to Christianity and eventually to make them citizens loyal to the Spanish crown.

But the founding of the missions in San Antonio had other purposes as well, including the establishment of a supply base and rest area en route to the missions in East Texas in an area near the Texas-Louisiana border known as Los Adaes.

When the French drove the Spaniards from East Texas, three of the missions in Los Adaes were moved to San Antonio.

The five missions established in San Antonio are currently known as The Alamo (formally Mission San Antonio de Valero), San Jose, Concepcion, San Francisco de la Espada and San Juan Capistrano.

In the context of the missions, the term "secularization" has been misunderstood by many historians. While it means converting something to non-religious purposes, it is also an ecclesiastical term that differentiates local, or secular, clergy who are under the authority of the bishop from religious orders of priests, such as the Franciscans, Redemptorists or Jesuits, who are directed by their own superiors.

The process of "secularization" of the missions involved turning them over to the secular diocesan priests at the end of the missionary period — normally intended to last 10 to 20 years — when the religious missionary priests were to move on to new unsettled frontiers.

Several decades after the missions were established in San Antonio, they went through "partial secularization" and "complete secularization."

Partial secularization, called doctrina, saw management of the mission lands and communities turned over to Indian converts as missionary priests remained and tended to the congregation's spiritual needs.

Complete secularization, called curato, occurred when a mission was completely turned over to secular church authorities and the religious priests left.[13]

Most of the local confusion over the terminology arose because in the 1790's, when the missions here were secularized, large parts of the extensive mission farm lands had already been turned over to the Indians as part of the mission plan to assimilate them into the larger community using skills learned at the mission.

When the missionary priests left, most of the churches were closed a short time later and their religious items taken to San Fernando Church. The parish inherited the five missions, but had no need for additional church buildings.

Then, the turmoil of the Mexican and then Texas revolutions confused international relations and boundaries. That left the titular owner of the mission churches in San Antonio, the Bishop of Monterrey, removed by more than great geographical distance from the churches. So, from before 1810 to long after 1845, they were mostly unused and fell into ruin.

In essence, secularization turned out to be neglect.

While the secular priests in San Antonio did not immediately need the newly acquired mission churches to serve the city's faithful, the chapels always remained church property until 1883 when the Alamo was sold to the State of Texas. The four other missions eventually were restored to full liturgical use.

MISSION SAN ANTONIO DE VALERO

Mission San Antonio de Valero was founded May 1, 1718, at a temporary site on the west side of the river. The mission was moved several times. A hurricane in 1724 demolished the structure. The mission's final move in 1727 was to its present location on the east bank of the river.

It is believed Mission San Antonio had at least five different sites.

Construction of the chapel we now recognize as the Alamo was begun in 1758.

The name "Alamo" means "cottonwood" in Spanish, a tree that grew in the state of Coahuila, Mexico. A town near the city of Parras in Coahuila was known as San Jose y Santiago del Alamo de Parras, shortened to Pueblo del Alamo. A flying company (mounted cavalry) from this town was stationed in San Antonio starting in 1803 for several years and eventually the garrison's location became known as "El Alamo."

In the 1700's, most soldiers lived on the west side of the river near the presidio on Military Plaza and had to ford the river at the Camino Real, now known as Commerce Street, to reach Mission San Antonio.

In 1736, a temporary bridge of six large beams was placed over the river. But when soldiers harassed Indian women living at the mission, the priest ordered the beams removed.

The governor, who was in residence at the presidio, promptly ordered the padre to replace the bridge. He refused, saying that his Indians were busy and could not be spared. The governor sent a group of soldiers to recruit enough Indians to replace the bridge.

However, the padre would not give up. He placed Indian guards on the bridge with orders not to let anyone cross, including the governor himself. This news enraged the governor and he gathered troops and charged toward the crossing. After crossing the bridge, the governor burst into the padre's office, uttered a few choice words, and informed the padre that he would see that he was sent back to Mexico.

Some time later, it was the governor who was removed, and, one suspects, the bridge was also.[14]

The Alamo was secularized in 1794, and like the other missions in San Antonio, was left under the care of San Fernando Parish. As the mission compound fell into disuse after secularization the church property on Alamo Plaza was mainly used by the military.

In 1806, part of the two-story administrative and office block later known as the Long Barracks, was turned into the city's first hospital.

The Battle of the Alamo on March 6, 1836, ended a 13-day siege. That battle began because in December of 1835, Texan forces had defeated Gen. Perfecto de Cos while some of his troops holed up in the old mission compound.

Cos was forced to sign surrender papers in a house in La Villita that today bears his name and he was sent to Mexico City in disgrace.

This enraged the general's brother-in-law, Gen. Antonio Lopez de Santa Anna, the president of Mexico who assumed dictatorial powers and named himself the "Napoleon of the West." He promptly marched on San Antonio to quell the growing rebellion among both new settlers and native citizens.

Cos had removed the ceiling of the chapel in the December battle to allow a ramp to be built to roll a cannon up to the top of the wall.

It is believed the original chapel had at least one bell tower similar to that at Mission San Jose. Others say it had two. Whatever the case, the building also suffered extensive damage during the Battle of the Alamo. After Santa Anna left town, forces that stayed behind had been ordered to destroy the walls or anything else that was left that might be used as a fortress.

The flattened compound walls, roofless and partially toppled walls of the chapel and burned out roofless ruin of the Long Barracks is what was found by Texans who returned to San Antonio after the Battle of San Jacinto on April 21, 1836, where Santa Anna was defeated by forces under Sam Houston and Texas won independence from Mexico.

The Alamo remained in ruins until 1850 when the U.S. government leased the property for use as a quartermaster's depot under the command of Army Maj. E.B. Babbitt.

The Army hired architect John Fries to make the building usable. He added stones atop the walls to make them even, added a roof and designed the baroque-shaped parapet above the main doors.

His design has since become an architectural hallmark copied in hundreds of buildings in Texas and elsewhere.

The chapel was purchased for $20,000 by the State of Texas on April 23, 1883, from Bishop John C. Neraz and placed under the custody of the City of San Antonio.

The barracks ruins next to the chapel and other adjacent property were purchased by Clara Driscoll for the Daughters of the Republic of Texas. The barracks and other property were finally purchased by the State of Texas and, in 1905, the Texas Legislature declared the Daughters of the Republic of Texas the official custodians of the Alamo.[15]

In 1978, the four other San Antonio missions, Concepcion, San Francisco de la Espada, San Jose and San Juan Capistrano were officially designated part of the San Antonio Missions National Historical Park.

Creation of the missions park required a unique church-state arrangement because the mission chapels are still in daily use as Catholic churches.

THE ALAMO IS A SHRINE TO TEXAS HEROES.
Convention and Visitors Bureau

FRANCISCAN MISSIONARIES ACCOMPANIED BY SPANISH SOLDIERS ESTABLISHED MISSIONS LIKE SAN JOSE AS SMALL CITIES WHERE THEY TAUGHT NATIVE INDIANS WORK SKILLS, HOW TO READ AND WRITE AND BAPTIZED THEM IN THE CATHOLIC FAITH.
Texas Highways Magazine

MISSION SAN FRANCISCO DE LA ESPADA IS THE SOUTHERNMOST OF SAN ANTONIO'S FIVE SPANISH COLONIAL MISSION CHURCHES.
Texas Highways Magazine

MISSION CONCEPCION'S STURDY DESIGN HELPED IT LAST AND BECOME THE NATION'S OLDEST UNRECONSTRUCTED CHURCH STILL IN USE.
Texas Highways Magazine

MISSION SAN JUAN CAPISTRANO WAS AMONG THREE MISSIONS HASTILY MOVED FROM EAST TEXAS TO SAN ANTONIO IN 1731.
Texas Highways Magazine

THE STONE ESPADA AQUEDUCT IS A HISTORIC LANDMARK WITHIN THE SAN ANTONIO MISSIONS NATIONAL HISTORICAL PARK.
National Park Service Photo

ORNATELY CARVED WINDOW AT SAN JOSE.
National Park Service

Physical maintenance of the church buildings and all parish activities are the responsibility of the Archdiocese of San Antonio. The National Park Service maintains and manages everything up to the front doors of the churches or chapels, including the extended grounds, ruins and structures not used for church purposes.

Continuing maintenance and restoration of the churches by the archdiocese is assisted by several community organizations, including the San Antonio Conservation Society and Los Compadres, a group founded to support all phases of the national historical park.

MISSION SAN JOSE

"Queen of the Missions of New Spain" is how Mission San Jose y San Miguel de Aguayo was described in a report to church authorities in Mexico City in the late 18th Century.

It is certainly that.

In fact, some royal visitors were as amazed and impressed with San Jose as its Franciscan designers had hoped the Indians would be.

Imagine their astonishment at coming across the open plains south of the mission and seeing for the first time the church's dome and open bell tower silhouetted against the bright, hot South Texas sky.

To see such exuberant and refined architecture and sculpture on the desolate provincial frontier stirred criticism from some — one priest dismissed it as "trifling" — but it usually inspired awe and wonder, being called everything from a miracle to devotional.

It is about seven and one-half miles south of Mission San Antonio. The Spaniards probably chose the site because of easy access to the water of the San Antonio River which originally came down an acequia from a small dam about two miles north, just downstream from Mission Concepcion.

By 1758, San Jose was described as having 84 apartments built of stone with flat roofs, parapets and loopholes. Each apartment had a metate (a stone to grind corn), a pot and other materials, including a comal, or flat metal or clay griddle, for cooking corn tortillas. Even swimming pools were available for both parishioners and the military.[16]

San Jose was partially secularized on July 23, 1794, its lands and possessions divided among the Indians who had lived there. By February 29, 1824, it was completely secularized. From 1859 to 1868, the Benedictine Fathers maintained a priory at the former mission. In the meantime, the foundations of the church weakened and, on December 10, 1868, part of the north wall collapsed. The dome and roof fell in December 25, 1874.

A new rectory was built in 1931 as restoration began in earnest. Reconstruction of San Jose was completed on April 18, 1937, and the church rededicated on that date. In 1941, it was declared a State and National Historical Site.

Today, San Jose is the most extensively restored compound and visitors can get a good idea of what the mission presence in Texas was all about.

MISSION CONCEPCION

Mission Nuestra Senora de la Purisima Concepcion (Our Lady of the Immaculate Conception) is the formal name of Mission Concepcion. It was initially located with two other missions in East Texas near the Angelina River. It moved to San Antonio with Missions San Juan Capistrano and San Francisco de la Espada on March 5, 1731.

Concepcion is, perhaps, the least-fanciful of the mission churches here. But it alone has endured while the others have collapsed; revealing, perhaps, the reason for such a square, severe, sturdy-looking structure. Concepcion has its church, but little else from its mission days.

Concepcion was partially secularized on August 1, 1794, and became a sub-mission of San Jose. By the spring of 1819, Mass was no longer offered in the church.

On February 29, 1824, it was closed, but remained largely intact. Today, Mission Concepcion is the oldest unreconstructed church in the United States still used for religious purposes.

The "Battle of Concepcion" between Texans and a Mexican army was fought near the mission on October 27, 1835. The Texans, under James Bowie, famed for the large knives that bear his name, won their first decisive victory in the Texas war for independence.

The Brothers of Mary of St.Mary's College downtown were caretakers of the mission from 1855 to 1911. In 1922, the Redemptorist Fathers began serving the mission.

Archbishop Robert E. Lucey's campaign to restore the missions included an invitation to the Franciscans to return to San Antonio to staff the missions founded 200 years earlier by their predecessors.

He always felt it seemed more appropriate to have the historic missions staffed by priests wearing long brown, hooded robes and white cord sashes.

Since creation of the national park, the city rerouted the street in front of the church, allowing an expansive grassy approach and unobtrusive visitor parking. A wooden pole fence had been near the front of the mission to shield the site from the street, which passed only yards from the front doors of the church. The realignment allowed the fence to be removed, providing a splendid view of the historic landmark.

In the 1920's, St. John's Seminary was built right behind the mission church, which served as the seminary chapel for a time. The seminary was closed and its buildings are now used by the Patrician Movement drug rehabilitation program and are fenced off from the mission.

Visitors to Concepcion had long been intrigued by the "Eye of God" on the ceiling of the convento room. But when the

MISSION ESPADA'S ORIENTAL-STYLE DOOR.
National Park Service

paintings were cleaned in 1988, a complete face with two eyes was found on the face of a sun that came peering through as old paint layers were removed. The cleaning was supervised by Paul Schwartzbaum, a member of the international oversight team for the restoration of Michaelangelo's frescoes in the Vatican's Sistine Chapel.

MISSION SAN FRANCISCO DE LA ESPADA

Most of the Spanish colonial missions had several locations and Mission San Francisco de la Espada was no exception.

It was once located on the Neches River near present day Neches in Houston County, moved to six miles west of present Alto in Cherokee County and, a year before moving to the banks of the San Antonio River, it was near Zilker Park in Austin.

Espada is a small building with unusual design details, such as a door opening with a large circular top that is almost Oriental in feeling.

But the real treasures of Espada are its dam and aqueduct. Together, they are the only Spanish colonial water system still functioning in the United States. In 1965, they were designated National Historical Landmarks.

The river waters had served this mission well, as its farm and ranch lands had been very productive, particularly from 1740 to 1780. A report by Franciscan teacher and historian Father Juan Augustin Morfi written in 1777-78, noted that 815 persons had been baptized since the mission's founding.[16]

On July 12, 1794, the mission was partially secularized and was completely secularized on February 29, 1824. From 1858 to 1907, the Rev. Francois Bouchu, a native of Sainte-Colombe-Vienne in southeastern France, served as pastor of Espada.

He wrote to relatives in France that he discovered two snakes hibernating under the small bells that are rung during the liturgy. One evening, as he reached for a book on a shelf, he grabbed a sleeping snake instead. Despite these distractions, Bouchu worked tirelessly at his ministry for several decades and, at age 78, died at Santa Rosa Hospital on August 19, 1907.[17]

Bouchu was followed by Claretian Fathers who oversaw Espada from San Juan Capistrano because the church at Espada was temporarily closed in 1909. After much-needed repair, the church was reopened in 1915. Further restoration was done in 1962. The Franciscans returned to Mission Espada in 1967.

MISSION SAN JUAN CAPISTRANO

Mission San Juan Capistrano was named San Jose de los Nazonis when a part of Los Adaes in East Texas. The name was changed when it was moved to San Antonio so as not to confuse it with already-established Mission San Jose y San Miguel de Aguayo. The chapel of San Juan was built about

100 yards from the San Antonio River. The building was made from a rough wooden base covered with heavy clay plaster.

Crops such as corn, beans, squash, grapes, melons, peppers, sweet potatoes and sugar cane were raised using the waters brought to the mission's extensive farmlands by a five-mile-long aqueduct system constructed in the 1730's. The mission was partially secularized on July 14, 1794, with complete secularization on February 29, 1824.

Serious repair of the church's west side was begun in 1907 and completed two years later. From 1923 to 1956, the Redemptorist Fathers oversaw the mission church. They were followed by diocesan or secular priests. Presently, the Franciscans at Mission Espada also serve this mission.

Restoration work on the walls, the interior of the church and the friary was done in the 1960's. [18,19]

Part of the park service's restoration of San Juan is to include an historic reconstruction of the mission's farm where crops will be raised and authentically costumed staff will demonstrate how the mission residents lived in the 1700's. The mission residents also had learned to forge iron and make pottery as well as items from wood, cloth and leather. Such handicrafts and skills also will be featured at the San Juan Demonstration Farm when it is completed and fully operational.

The San Antonio River played a major role in the success the missions experienced and today the four missions remain a spectacular legacy of the grandeur of Spain's ambitions in the New World, even along the remote frontiers of Texas.

THE ACEQUIAS

Construction of the acequias began shortly after Mission San Antonio de Valero (The Alamo) was established in 1718.

Acequia is an Arabic word for a ditch or canal that carries water. The word was introduced to the Spanish language when the Moors invaded Iberia. Moorish watermasters were proficient in developing water distribution channels. They had a system that classified more than 225 topographical slopes. Areas of land were evaluated in terms of quantities of water that were a part of property rights. Acequias have a long history as a means of dispersing water in semi-arid lands in Arabia and Spain and, as it turned out, in Texas. [20]

The Acequia Madre that served Mission San Antonio and its lands was about five miles long and at one time supplied water to 600 acres of mission property.

It received its water from the headwaters of the San Antonio River and followed natural land contours for six miles through what is now downtown San Antonio. Several sections remain, one at the Alamo (the goldfish pond), another at HemisFair Park and a third at Brackenridge Park. The one in the Alamo Gardens under the care of the Daughters of the Republic of Texas is, however, done in very non-historic concrete.

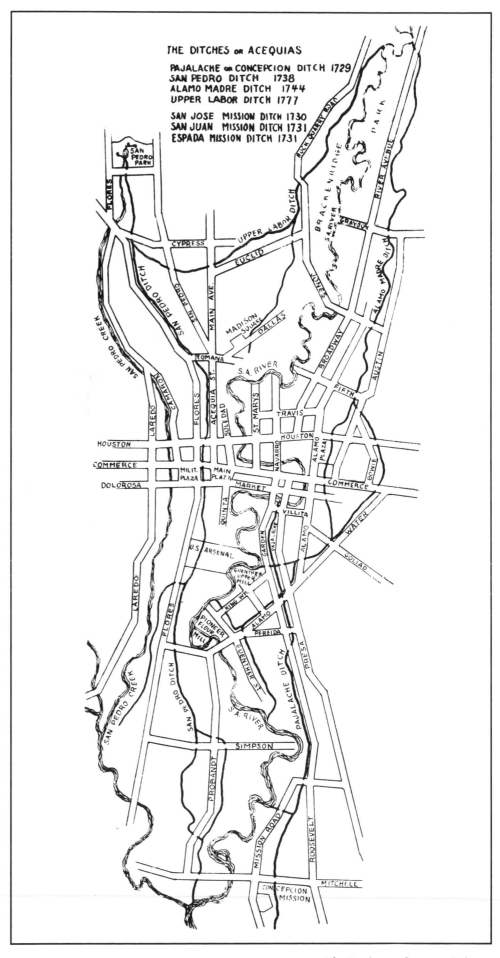

THE DITCHES or ACEQUIAS

PAJALACHE or CONCEPCION DITCH 1729
SAN PEDRO DITCH 1738
ALAMO MADRE DITCH 1744
UPPER LABOR DITCH 1777

SAN JOSE MISSION DITCH 1730
SAN JUAN MISSION DITCH 1731
ESPADA MISSION DITCH 1731

The Institute of Texan Cultures

Water in the acequia's southern section originated from the San Antonio River just below its juncture with San Pedro Creek. It was about five miles long and flowed south to the missions. It supplied water for domestic animals, large acreage of farm land and powered a gristmill near the mission.

The gristmill has been restored and can be seen at Mission San Jose.

Constant failure of a diversion dam caused this acequia to be abandoned in the latter half of the 19th century.

The Concepcion Acequia was built around 1729 or 1730 about one year before Mission Concepcion was established. It took water from a dam built on Presa (Spanish for Dam) Street near today's Hertzberg Circus Museum and then flowed south to Mission Concepcion. This acequia, the largest in the area, had many laterals for irrigating farm lands.

In 1869, Concepcion Dam was removed and no visible trace of the acequia remains, although sections are known to be under surface dirt.

In 1731, water began flowing in the San Juan Acequia toward Mission San Juan Capistrano. This acequia started on the east side of the river opposite Mission San Jose. It was abandoned in the 1920's but re-opened in the 1960's, restored and today is operational and providing irrigation water to farm fields south of San Antonio.

Construction of the Espada Acequia started in 1731 and was completed around 1745. This acequia provided water for Mission Espada and was abandoned in the 1880's. It was renovated and re-opened in 1895 and continues to provide water for irrigation.

Acequia Park includes Espada Dam and much of the Espada Canal. This acequia continues to take its water from behind Espada Dam south of downtown next to Mission Burial Park. It is the only functioning Spanish colonial dam and aqueduct system in the United States.

In 1965, the United States Department of Interior designated Espada Aqueduct as a registered National Historical Landmark. In 1976, the Bexar Chapter of the Texas Society of Professional Engineers placed a monument with a bronze plaque to honor the early builders of the acequias.

The Upper Labor Acequia began operating in 1781, flowing from the San Antonio River headwaters in a southerly direction, joining the San Pedro Acequia near what is now West Laurel Avenue.

This acequia still takes its water from behind a small dam in Brackenridge Park, flows about 50 yards in the zoo and is eventually diverted into the old water works channel.

Approximately 250 yards of the acequia is still intact and can be seen in a field opposite the Sunken Gardens in Brackenridge Park. And a good-sized portion of the acequia is currently being used in the zoo's waterfowl area.

The San Pedro Acequia was put into use in about 1735, drawing water from San Pedro Springs. It followed the wa-

THE ORIGINAL DAM FOR THE ACEQUIA SERVING MISSION ESPADA STILL DIVERTS SAN ANTONIO RIVER WATER TO FARMLAND NEAR THE SPANISH COLONIAL MISSION BUILT IN 1731. THE ACEQUIAS SERVED AS THE CITY WATER SYSTEM FOR 200 YEARS.
The Institute of Texan Cultures

THE CURVING CHANNEL ATOP THE ESPADA AQUEDUCT IS PART OF THE ACEQUIA SYSTEM STILL USED TO IRRIGATE FARM LANDS.
The Institute of Texan Cultures

tershed between the San Antonio River and San Pedro Creek and was four miles long. Its path followed present-day North Flores Street and served the very heart of Villa de San Fernando around Main Plaza, continued southward and emptied into the river a short distance above the mouth of San Pedro Creek.

This acequia furnished drinking water to the city while San Pedro Creek and the river were used for bathing and washing clothes, buggies and horses.

The acequia ceased to be used after 1906. Parts of it remain visible today at the Bexar County Justice Center on Main Plaza and the San Antonio Housing Authority headquarters complex on South Flores Street.

The Alazan Acequia, sometimes referred to as the Alazan Ditch, was the last acequia built in San Antonio, being completed in late 1876. It took water from the San Pedro Springs at a juncture with the Upper Labor Acequia and flowed westward in line with West Ashby Place to the Missouri Pacific tracks and then southward parallel with the tracks, crossed Fredericksburg Road, turned toward Colorado Street, then eventually along Frio street and emptied into the river near Tampico Street. Unfortunately, no traces of this acequia remain visible.

In all, the Spaniards and Indians from the missions built more than 15 miles of major acequias that provided water to the villa, the five mission compounds and irrigated at least 3,500 acres of farmland.

On December 6, 1975, Jack Beretta addressed the Society of Colonial Wars at La Mansion del Rio Hotel.

Mr. Beretta finished high school in San Antonio and graduated from the Massachusetts Institute of Technology in 1923 receiving a degree in architectural engineering.

He had served as president of the National Society of Professional Engineers for two years. His account of how the acequias were built and his evaluation of them is preserved in the archives of the San Antonio Conservation Society.

He began by informing his audience that there were no records available of how the actual staking out of the acequias took place, more specifically, that there were no records of how they performed the engineering and construction of the acequias. He pointed out the grades of the acequias vary from 18 inches to the mile to 43 inches to the mile, which provided a delicate flow to avoid erosion.

His explanation of how they were engineered was as follows:

"What they used was a large triangle built of timber. And, from the apex of this triangle, they hung plumb bobs. The bottom leg of this triangle was scaled into gradients.

"The location of the acequias was done roughly by eye, which had to follow certain natural grades. Then they would adjust the slope of it according to the number of gradients to provide the necessary slope.

"They did not have transits or levels or modern engineering tools. They did it with the eye and with this primitive engineering tool."[21]

As an engineer, Mr. Beretta was, no doubt, fascinated with the outstanding engineering work done during this early period of our history. The acequias do, indeed, represent a remarkable period of San Antonio's history and should remind all that the remnants of these waterways are one of the earliest examples of a planned water supply and irrigation system in the United States.

AQUADORES TO ARTESIAN WELLS

When San Antonio was in its infancy, water was delivered to users by "aquadores." Buckets of water taken from the San Antonio River and San Pedro Springs were hung on each end of a yoke placed across the shoulders of men known as aquadores. How long this method of delivering water was used is not fully known. But once the acequias were built, the aquador was the water master in charge of the gates directing water down the proper channel to the city, into houses, the missions, to irrigate farmland or water livestock.

In fact, it was illegal to use the water from acequias for anything but household use as early as 1776 when an edict issued January 21st by the Alcalde (Mayor) of San Fernando de Bexar stated: "No clothing should be laundered in the acequia of the villa . . . . Failure to comply will result in confiscation of the clothing."[22]

Some have noted that the San Antonio River was the city's bathtub until the establishment of a waterworks in the late 1800's. Bathhouses became so popular that most families living on the river banks owned one. Those who could not afford one formed partnerships with their neighbors and shared them.

They were little more than wooden frames covered with canvas and floated on pontoons made of empty barrels. Around the sides of the canvas coverings, seats were placed for bathers to use for changing clothing. Floors that extended a short distance from the seats allowed the bather to enter the water or emerge.

Bathing parties were the in thing. Women and children had them in the afternoons after their siestas, while the men customarily bathed at night or early morning. The first public bathhouse was in the river just south of Navarro and Market Streets. A public bathhouse at San Pedro Springs was very popular because of its natural rock bottom.

The river was also used to wash and clean many items. It was not unusual to observe wagons pulled by horses or mules into shallow spots along the river to be cleaned. Unfortunately, the possibillity of contamination was extremely high and a cholera epidemic in 1866 convinced city leaders that a sanitary method of delivering water to homes was necessary.

THE RIVER SERVED AS THE CITY LAUNDRY FOR DECADES, AS SHOWN HERE AS TWO WOMEN POUND CLOTHES ON THE RIVER BANK.
The Grandjean Collection SAR 180, DRT Library

By 1878, La Coste Co. had built a water delivery system, later to be known as the Water Works, that used surface water from a reservoir constructed on a hill near the eastern end of Mahncke Park near where the Botanical Center and Halsell Conservatory are today.

However, not all San Antonians were ready for a change. It seemed many had difficulty in visualizing how a modern water system operated and if it was really needed. After all, the first brewery had been built in 1855 by C. Degen and there were about 20 saloons open at all hours.

In 1857, plain whiskey was only 5 cents a drink and if you wanted ice, it cost only 10 cents more! Perhaps this is the time when one could hear, "Plain water rusts your pipes! Bring us another branch water and bourbon."

However, another incident may have changed the minds of many about the value of a water works. In the early 1800's, acequias supplied water to most parts of the city and residents were content with their water supply.

Then, on March 9, 1840, an Indian raid resulting in the deaths of several Indians delighted a physician and surgeon named Dr. Weidemann.

Mrs. M. A. Maverick was visiting a Mrs. Higginbotham when Dr. Weidemann appeared outside their window and placed a freshly severed Indian head on the sill. He bowed courteously and said: "With your permission, madam" and disappeared.

Shortly, he returned with another head and explained that he had examined all the dead Indians and had selected these specimens of a male and female and, in addition, had two entire bodies to preserve as skeletons.

Soon, he appeared with a cart and removed the two heads from the window sill and departed with his cargo.

That night, reported Mrs. Maverick, he "stewed the bodies in a soap boiler and when the flesh was completely desiccated, emptied the cauldron into the acequia" that supplied drinking water for the residents.

Several days later, when citizens realized what had happened to their water, they mobbed the mayor's office and demanded that Dr. Weidemann be arrested. When brought to trial he was called "diablo," "demonio" and "sin verguenza." He was convicted and fined and left the courtroom laughing, "the Indians had all sailed by in the night."[23]

Despite this experience, change still took time and it wasn't until 1883 when the Water Works was sold to George Brackenridge that the city began moving toward an underground pipe system to distribute water.

Brackenridge remained president of the company until 1906. Under his leadership, wells were dug to supply the city. He aggressively purchased property in different areas of the city for well sites. By the time he sold the water works, several artesian wells were in use.

In 1899, the Water Works Company deeded to the city the land the company acquired along the banks of the river near its headwaters off Broadway in what is now Brackenridge Park. The deed stipulated that the city could keep the title as long as the land was used as a public park. A similar deed was issued for the area known as Mahncke Park.

The San Antonio Water Works was bought and sold a number of times. In fact, it once belonged to a syndicate in Antwerp, but after World War I a group of local investors purchased it. The Water Works became a publicly owned utility in 1925, functioning as the City Water Board.

In 1992, the Water Board was merged with the City Public Works Department's Wastewater Treatment Division and the newly created Alamo Conservation and Water Re-Use District to become the San Antonio Water System with jurisdiction over all water use, treatment, reuse and disposal.

BEFORE A FLEET OF RIVER BARGES WAS PUT INTO USE, SPECIAL CRAFT LIKE THIS CASA RIO GONDOLA WERE USED BY RIVER BUSINESSES. HERE, DELEGATES TO AN EPSILON SIGMA ALPHA CONVENTION IN THE EARLY 1950'S ENJOY A RIDE DOWN THE RIVER.
The Institute of Texan Cultures

CHAPTER THREE

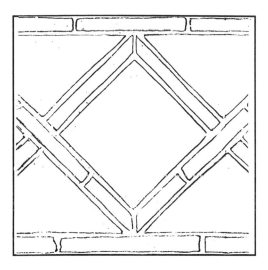

The River And Its People

A city has its roots in many facets of its history.

In San Antonio, the river has become the flowing ribbon tying together the many people who have lived here. More than that, the river has linked the traditions and mores of its inhabitants.

Those who first came here over 300 years ago were impressed with the potential of development around the banks of the San Antonio River and the San Pedro Springs. At that time, the winding stream was described as paradise in its natural state, untouched by human interference. It was and is an alluring place that is not easily forgotten, and has an almost magical attraction that draws people back to its banks.

The burning question then, and one that remains now, is how to properly use such a place.

The Indians used it in many pragmatic ways: As a campsite, for drinking, washing and preparing foods. It served them well. The Spanish saw it as a place that would support a villa and even a city. The mission priests saw its chief value as supporting farm lands and livestock necessary for people to survive.

Later settlers almost immediately recognized the commercial potential the river offered.

All focused on the usefulness of the river. Although their agendas may have been somewhat different, their goals and aspirations were centered on the river's abundant supply of fresh water.

During the Spanish colonial era, the settlements were first composed of three entities — friars and Indians, Mexican soldier-settlers and Canary Islanders. But the hardships of frontier life and the threat of hostile Indians forged them all into an integrated community one. Out of this unified society grew the tradition of a culture that is diverse and ever changing.

When these various groups interacted and exchanged traditions, their cultures blended to produce a subtle cosmopolitan blend that has become an almost intangible something that makes San Antonio special[25]

Fiestas and holidays linked to the Mexican period in Texas are major celebrations in present day San Antonio. The Diez y Seis de Septiembre (Sixteenth of September) the date on which Mexico — and thus, Texas —proclaimed independence from Spain in 1820. It is the equivalent of the Fourth of July and observed with some of the biggest Diez y Seis ceremonies and festivities of Mexico, including the annual re-enactment of the "Grito" or cry for independence.

The town council of San Antonio, by the way, was the only government entity in New Spain to officially endorse Hidalgo's cry for independence.

That gesture, in the form of a formal resolution, got the president of the town council summoned to Mexico City where the viceroy had him beheaded.

Cinco de Mayo (May 5) celebrates the defeat of invading French forces at Puebla, Mexico, in 1862, a victory won under the leadership of Texas-born Gen. Ignacio Zaragoza.

Christmas celebrations seen along the river and its environs include those of Spanish and Mexican origin, as well as one that could only happen in San Antonio because of its River Walk.

Los Pastores is celebrated at Christmas and is a medieval spectacle brought to San Antonio during the Spanish colonial period. It is a morality play in which the main characters are the Christmas shepherds beset by devils and other nefarious characters but the shepherds are protected by St. Michael the Archangel.

Las Posadas commemorates the journey of Mary and Joseph to Bethlehem and the family's search for lodging so Mary can give birth.

Crowds of people line the River Walk to follow the costumed Joseph, Mary and an accompanying retinue of shepherds, angels and more. The people carry candles and sing carols in Spanish as they accompany the Holy Family in their search. The procession stops three times along the River Walk seeking hospitality. At the final stop in La Villita, where the travelers are offered a manger, hot chocolate and other refreshments are served.

The procession's way along the River Walk is lighted by luminarias, small white paper sacks weighted with sand that holds lighted candles inside. The closely spaced string of luminarias is placed along the river edge of the walks by the San Antonio Conservation Society.

Las Posadas is just one part of San Antonio's annual Christmas festivities on the River Walk, which are among the most beautiful in the country.

The city strings lights in the towering trees along the River Walk and the Paseo del Rio Association recruits sponsors for holiday floats that are decorated with Christmas lights and have live music. The city Christmas tree on Alamo Plaza also is lighted to help launch the city's annual Christmas celebrations.

More than 100,000 San Antonians and visitors crowd downtown and the River Walk on the night that the plaza tree is lighted, the River Walk lights are turned on and the Holiday River Parade is staged.

The River Walk, already a visual delight, becomes an incredible, breathtaking spectacle of twinkling lights, luminarias, lighted floats, choirs and more, all of which are duplicated in shimmering reflections on the river's water.

The Holiday River Parade was started modestly in 1982 and has become one of the biggest events in the city, attracting visitors from around the world who want to experience the splendor of San Antonio's unique Christmas celebration on the river.

One year, the Christmas festivities were abruptly interrupted when a River Walk resident called the city Park Rangers complaining that "Santa Claus" was shouting "Ho! Ho! Ho!"

NATURAL BEAUTY OF THE RIVER WALK IS SEEN HERE AS A BARGE PASSES UNDER THE GRACEFUL NAVARRO STREET BRIDGE.
David Anthony Richelieu

LAS POSADAS CHRISTMAS PROCESSION PASSES BY UNDER GLITTERING RIVER WALK LIGHTS AS RIVER BARGE DINERS LOOK ON.
Texas Highways Magazine

COLORFULLY DRESSED MARIACHIS SERENADE DINERS ON A RIVER BARGE IN WHAT HAS BECOME THE TRADITIONAL RIVER WALK STYLE.
Texas Highways Magazine

THE RIVER WALK'S BREATHTAKING CHRISTMAS LIGHTING AND SHIMMERING REFLECTIONS ATTRACT HUGE CROWDS TO DOWNTOWN.
Texas Highways Magazine

CANDLES GLOW WARMLY AT LAS POSADAS
Texas Highways Magazine

too loudly to the festive holiday crowds and even annoying the pet cat.

The Park Rangers promptly did their duty and approached the shouting Santa, only to discover that under the costume was an assistant director of the city Parks Department — and one of their bosses.

The Blessing of the Animals is a tradition in San Antonio in which a priest asks for the good health of the animal so that it will serve its master.

San Fernando Cathedral is among churches that regularly blesses the animals.

The historic cathedral also stages the Way of the Cross on Good Friday. A crowd gathers in Market Square to see Christ condemned to death by Pontius Pilate and then follows him as he carries his cross through the streets to the front of the cathedral where he is to be crucified.

Thousands attend the cathedral's Good Friday procession and many have proudly served in the drama for years, their roles revered as family heirlooms.

Another Mexican religious observance is the Day of the Dead, or All Souls' Day, in which Death is mocked by waxen and candy skulls, skeletons and other hand-made macabre figures, some of which appear on or as pastries, bread and other baked goods.

The banks of the San Antonio River also can be heard echoing many weekends with conjunto music that features a lead accordion accompanied by drum, cornet, saxophone, guitars, and, most recently, tubas.

The popular dance music is a cultural fusion of Mexican rhythms and instruments with polkas and other dances from Central Europe. Conjunto, especially with its latest addition of tuba, sounds remarkably like German folk music done with a fast Mexican beat.

Another music festival, the Gran Baile, features Mexican bands playing a variety of Latin music, including conjunto music. Of course, mariachis can be heard nightly on the San Antonio River.[26]

During the summer, Mexican folkloric dancers and singers are showcased several times a week on the stage of the Arneson River Theater.

Add to all this, the traditions of anglos from a variety of backgrounds and you sense the kaleidoscopic cultural diversity that has thrived along the banks of the San Antonio River.

During the Mexican Era in San Antonio, from 1821 to 1836, settlers came from the newly formed United States and their numbers increased dramatically after the defeat of the Mexican Army at San Jacinto.

The influx of Germans began in 1845. German scientist Ferdinand Roemer estimated that the population of San Antonio was slightly above 800 people between 1845 and 1847. By 1860, the population reached over 8,200. Roemer had this to say about San Antonio and its river around 1845:

IN 1936, FIESTA SAW A DAYTIME RIVER PARADE. CROWDS GATHERED ON THE ST. MARY'S STREET BRIDGE AND ON THE BANKS BY THE SAN ANTONIO DRUG CO. OPPOSITE THE TOWER LIFE BUILDING TO ENJOY THIS NEW KIND OF FRIVOLITY ON THE RIVER.
The Institute of Texan Cultures

"On the following morning, we first visited the ruins of the old fort Alamo, which played such an important role in the War of Independence of Texas. The ruins as well as several other houses are on the left bank of the San Antonio River, whereas by far the greater part of the city is on the right bank.

"To reach this place we crossed the river over a wooden bridge which, like the rest of the city . . . showed unmistakable signs of neglect. The river is a beautiful stream as clear as the Comal (a river in New Braunfels about 30 miles from San Antonio) and of considerable depth and volume."[27]

What many called "German Town" extended from Alamo Plaza to the King William area and from South Water Street to South Flores. Notable buildings included the Menger Hotel, Beethoven Hall, the German-English School, St. Joseph's Catholic Church, the Turnverein German Athletic Club and St. John's Lutheran Church.

In present day San Antonio, the King William Historic District south of downtown with its many restored mansions and homes represents what is left of "German Town."

As with the Spanish and the Tejanos, the Germans brought their traditions to San Antonio, especially in music. They frequently celebrated musical saengerfests, and other activities, such as hunting parties, picnics, athletic meets, kaffee clatches with springerle cakes, and enjoyed beer gardens and multitudes of brass bands.

The Germans gathered at Main Plaza at Christmas time and, standing around fires from tar barrels, sang "O Stille Nacht" and "O Tannenbaum." Then they would serenade their neighbors, especially those who invited them in for Rhine wine and other refreshments.[28]

Beethoven Hall was built in 1895 by the Beethoven Mannerchor, a German men's singing chorus founded in 1867 and still active today. Beethoven Hall burned at least twice, but the worst damage came when its Imperial German facade was mindlessly shaved off in a street widening before HemisFair and replaced with a flat brick front.

The Liederkranz, another German singing society organized in the late 1800's, also flourishes today. In 1876, with a total population of over 17,000 in San Antonio, Germans and Alsatians were in the majority.

When the influx of Germans made it clear they needed their own church, efforts by the Catholic bishop to restore the Alamo chapel to use as a church were thwarted by the U.S. Army, which had leased the ruins from the bishop for use as a quartermaster's depot and built the now-famous facade to replace the destroyed original.

The federal troops had only recently returned to San Antonio after the Civil War and resumed their use of the Alamo, so they weren't anxious to go searching for new facilities.

Between 1870 and 1875, the city acquired 92 acres of land and gave them to the government for what today is Fort Sam Houston.

CRAWFISH HAVE BEEN FOUND IN THE RIVER. JAMES MORALES SHOWS OFF ONE HE CAUGHT IN 1926 NEAR ROOSEVELT PARK. THERE IS STILL FISHING TODAY IN THE RIVER, EVEN IN DOWNTOWN.
The Institute of Texan Cultures

A FINE CATCH, MRS. R.E. GOODSPEED POSES WITH THIS 1.5 POUND CRAWFISH FOUND NEAR PIONEER FLOUR MILLS BY HER BROTHER-IN-LAW, WHO WAS A NEWSPAPER PHOTOGRAPHER.
The Institute of Texan Cultures

FIESTA IS CELEBRATED AT CASA RIO RESTAURANT WHEN COATS AND TIES AND DRESSES AND HATS WERE USUAL PARTY ATTIRE.
Casa Rio Photo

EARLY RIVER PARADE FLOATS WERE DECORATED CANOES, LIKE THIS PIONEER FLOUR MILLS ENTRY TRIMMED WITH FLOWERS.
The Institute of Texan Cultures

THE BLOCK OF RESTORED BUILDINGS JUST WEST OF THE COMMERCE STREET BRIDGE INCLUDES THE SCHULTZE HARDWARE STORE THAT IS NOW A RESTAURANT. MAX SCHULTZE IS THE SECOND MAN FROM THE RIGHT.
Photo from Walter Schultze

AFTER INITIAL FLOOD-CONTROL WORK, THE RIVER WALK WAS STILL A DREAM, BUT THE RIVER BECAME NAVIGABLE BY CANOE.
The Institute of Texan Cultures

VIEW NORTH TO THE CROCKETT STREET BRIDGE AMID THE RIVER'S DENSE NATURAL FOLIAGE.   *The Institute of Texan Cultures*

THE SAME CROCKETT STREET CROSSING SHOWING THE CHANDLER BUILDING, RIGHT, AND SOME EARLY RIVER CHANNEL WORK.
San Antonio Express-News Photo

VIEW NORTH TO CROCKETT STREET SHOWS ORIGINAL MEXICAN RESTAURANT ARBOR, RIGHT, AND LOSOYA BUILDING BEYOND.
Photo from Jimmy Gause

CASINO CLUB DOMINATES CROCKETT CROSSING BEFORE **WPA** WORK.
Photo from Jimmy Gause

THIS PEACEFUL STRETCH OF RIVER AT THE NAVARRO STREET BRIDGE IS WHERE THE NIX HOSPITAL WAS BUILT ON THE RIGHT.

San Antonio Express-News Photo

ST. JOSEPH'S CHURCH, CALLED ST. JOSKE'S.

But Army use of the Alamo forced the German Catholics to build a new church just south of Alamo Plaza on Commerce Street. The cornerstone for St. Joseph's Church was laid in 1868 and the German gothic stone structure boasts of stained glass windows from Munich and murals of the Annunciation and Assumption that were painted by its first pastor, Father Henry Pefferkorn.

Over the decades, the street next to St. Joseph's connecting Commerce to Alamo Plaza was closed. The Joske's Bros. department store grew until, by the late 1960's, it was a 550,000 square-foot four-story mammoth covering the entire city block — minus the niche on its south side where St. Joseph's stands.

Because of that, for years, St. Joseph's was affectionately nicknamed, "St. Joske's." But its heritage remains unmistakable. The cornerstone and other original fixtures all bear inscriptions in German, not English or Latin.

In the early 1990's, a German Heritage Park was established on old Goliad Street at the Alamo Street entry to HemisFair Park and across from the original German-English School, now a hotel conference center.

Beethoven Hall is part of the heritage park and is to be restored as part of the master plan. Several stores and large homes built during the city's German immigrant period also will be restored and used as restaurants, shops and trade offices. Centerpiece of the complex will be a new Bierhalle and Garten adjacent to Beethoven Hall.

The Irish also came to San Antonio in large numbers, settling in what was known as Irish Flats, an area extending from near Alamo Plaza, north to Sixth Street and east of Broadway. Most of the original homes have been replaced by freeways and businesses.

The local Harp and Shamrock Society continues the traditions of the Irish. On St. Patrick's Day, the society sponsors a river parade of barges filled with officials of the local society, bagpipers and special guests who go gliding down the river while dyeing its water vivid green. City Council issues a proclamation officially changing the river's name to River Shannon for the day.

The city's biggest bash each year is the 10-day-long Fiesta San Antonio that celebrates the April 21, 1836, victory at San Jacinto that won Texas its independence from Mexico.

Fiesta includes more than 100 events. Among them are the "Battle of Flowers Parade" that began as the celebration for a visit to the city April 20, 1891, by President Benjamin Harrison and also to observe San Jacinto Day.

Rain canceled the parade and a few soaked bystanders saw the president. But on April 24, the city's best-dressed women circled Alamo Plaza in their open carriages "battling" one another with tossed flowers.

Another of Fiesta's parades has, as someone observed years ago, floats that really float — down the river.

The first night river parade was sponsored by the San Antonio Conservation Society in 1940. In 1941, the Texas Cava-

BEFORE THE ROUND TURRET OF THE CLIFFORD BUILDING APPEARED, THE COMMERCE STREET CROSSING WAS FAR LESS IMPOSING.
The Institute of Texan Cultures

LOOKING NORTH TOWARD THE CROCKETT STREET BRIDGE BEFORE THE FAMED CASINO CLUB OCCUPIED THE RIVER'S LEFT BANK.
The Institute of Texan Cultures

COMMERCE STREET AT THE RIVER WITH THE DULLNIG BUILDING'S DOMED CUPOLA INTACT BEFORE A STREET-WIDENING REMOVED IT. A SIGN ON THE TOBACCO STORE SAYS: 'TO WIN A PRIZE, GET YOUR LOTTERY TICKET AT MARY'S CIGAR STORE.'
San Antonio Conservation Society Photo

LOOKING SOUTH TOWARD THE COMMERCE STREET BRIDGE AT WHAT IS NOW THE BUSIEST SECTION OF THE RIVER WALK. TODAY AN ARCHED BRIDGE CROSSES THE RIVER ABOUT WHERE THE MAN IS WALKING ALONG THE RIGHT BANK. *Photo from Jimmy Gause*

STREETCARS CROSS THE COMMERCE STREET BRIDGE, PROBABLY IN THE EARLY 1920s. THE CASA RIO RESTAURANT SITE IS AT THE LEFT. THE SQUARE OPENINGS ABOVE THE STREETCAR ARE AT THE ORIGINAL MEXICAN RESTAURANT. *Casa Rio Photo*

STATUE ON THE COMMERCE STREET BRIDGE.
Ruben Alfaro Photo

liers, a local social club, took over sponsorship of the event. It now attracts more than 100,000 people to the River Walk to see the lighted and decorated floats that cruise down the river carrying various dignitaries and celebrities while bands, dancers and other entertainers on board excite onlookers.

The city's French celebrate Bastille Day. Chinese New Year's also is observed.

San Antonio is proud of its multicultural heritage and has maintained many traditions of the ethnic and immigrant groups who have so enriched the city and its history. Almost all flourished along the river.

THE COMMERCE STREET BRIDGE

In many ways, activities around the Commerce Street Bridge, located at Commerce and Losoya, reflect the historical diversity of San Antonio.

In 1736, it was called the Padre's Bridge (the Padre at the Alamo) and was made of six large beams. A more substantial bridge was built in 1803, but was destroyed by a flood in 1819.

In 1836, some referred to a footbridge of planks as Santa Anna's Bridge because it was strategically important for attacking the Alamo. Other wooden bridges were built across this busy and historical place, only to be destroyed by floods.

One of the wooden bridges spanning the river in the 1870's that best symbolized the cultural mix of San Antonio contained a warning sign in three languages. In German, Spanish, and in English it stated: "Walk your horse across the bridge or you will be fined!" In the 1870's, it was often called Lanier's Bridge for the poet Sidney Lanier who spent considerable time in San Antonio. Fascinated by the view of the river and its environs at this site, he observed in the oft-quoted San Antonio de Bexar:

"One may take one's stand on the Commerce Street Bridge and involve oneself in the life that goes by this way and that. Yonder comes a long train of enormous, blue-bodied covered wagons, built high and square in the stern, much like a fleet of Dutch galleons, and lumbering in a ponderous way that suggests cargos of silver and gold. These are drawn by fourteen mules each who are harnessed in four tiers . . . . Yonder fares slowly another train of wagons, drawn by great wide-horned oxen, whose evident tendency to run to hump and foreshoulder irresistibly persuades one of their cousinship to the buffalo.

"And now, as we leave the bridge in the gathering twilight and loiter down the street, we pass all manner of odd personages and 'characters.' Here hobbles an old Mexican who looks like old Father Time in reduced circumstances. There goes a little German boy who was captured a year ago by Indians. Here is a great Indian fighter . . . . there a portly, handsome buccaneer-looking captain, and so on, through a perfect gauntlet of people who have odd histories, odd natures or odd appearances."[29]

O. Henry reportedly stood at this bridge and on others in the early 1890's when formulating one of his memorable stories, "A Fog in San Antone." In 1895, the novelist Stephen Crane leaped from the Commerce Street Bridge to save a drowning girl.

This incident reminded Charles O. Kilpatrick, editor and publisher of the San Antonio Express-News for over 40 years, of "the man who got stuck in the mud."

In the early 1950's, a police officer was chasing a man down Commerce Street who jumped into the San Antonio River from the south side of the Commerce Street Bridge and landed in the river directly in front of Casa Rio Restaurant. The police officer stopped running and slowly made his way to the nearest telephone. A witness to this event asked, "Why aren't you going after the criminal?" The police officer quietly answered, "He's not going anywhere, he's stuck in the mud."

Sure enough, when other police officers arrived, they tossed him a rope and pulled him to shore. The river was shallow in 1950's due to a severe and prolonged drought; but, fortunately, when Stephen Crane jumped into the river, it was much deeper.

An iron bridge that was brought in by rail in 1877 replaced the wooden bridge in 1880. In 1914, a concrete bridge replaced the iron span, which was moved to Johnson Street in the King William area.

The concrete bridge, still in use, contains a most interesting concrete sculpture of a 6-foot-tall Indian warrior, framed by an arch, and facing Commerce Street.

The figure has a full headdress and is holding saucers in each hand from which water once gushed forth. The figure wears a breechcloth, moccasins and a bear-claw necklace. On each side are corn-stalk decorations.

The piece was designed as a drinking fountain and cost about $1,000. It was vandalized just three days after its installation in 1914 and its water connections were never repaired. Over the years, a large part of the left basin was damaged, but it was recently repaired.

This handsome Indian statue was commissioned by the San Antonio Express and was designed by Waldine Tauch and named by her as "First Inhabitant."

A native of Schulenburg, Texas, Ms. Tauch lived in San Antonio and studied with Pompeo Coppini who designed the Cenotaph on Alamo Plaza commissioned by the State of Texas to honor the defenders of the Alamo on the 100th anniversary of the battle. The model for Ms. Tauch's sculpture was said to be a "full-blooded" Indian who had wandered into San Antonio, posed for the artwork, and was never seen again.

Ms. Tauch received commissions for many other works of art, including the Le Seuer Smith Fountain in New York of four children whose great-grandfather was Gen. Victor C.B. Girardey of the Confederate Army, a war memorial in Bedford, Indiana, the "Gulf Breeze" at San Antonio's Witte Museum, and a bust of Mrs. Eli Hertzberg.

She and Coppini collaborated on a statue of Oscar Hammerstein placed in the Hammerstein Theater in New York.

The Coppini Academy still exists in San Antonio.[30]

Today, the Commerce Street Bridge is a major entryway to the River Walk for millions of visitors.

As Sidney Lanier did over 100 years ago, one can stand on this bridge and observe the flow of traffic that includes people from all walks of life, as well as interesting groups of people from other countries and the colorful individuals who add so much to the allure of the River Walk.

Along and near the banks of the San Antonio River in the late 1800's and early 1900's, one could find, for example, steak dinners with wine in 1874 that cost 40 cents.

In 1859, C.H. Guenther built a mill at the present-day site of Pioneer Flour Mills with the help of members of the Castro Colony in Medina County.

The Castro Colony was mostly Alsatian settlers who agreed to help build the mill on the San Antonio River to help market farm products raised on their land around what today is Castroville, about 30 miles west of San Antonio. Water wheels for the mill were made of native wood, as were the driving gears, but the millstone was imported from France.

During his lifetime, Guenther built other mills on the San Antonio River. The Guenther House, now on the grounds of the Pioneer complex, has been restored and is a popular bakery and restaurant.

The first train arrived in San Antonio in 1877, and a celebration was held on Bowen's Island. In 1878, water carts were used for street sprinkling and wild turkeys (not the drinking kind) sold for 25 cents.

The first public high school opened and the first telephone lines were installed in 1879. In 1880, Buffalo Bill entertained at the Casino Club and chili stands were open at night on Alamo Plaza. Oscar Wilde gave a lecture and the first annual Volkfest was held in 1882.

Train service to San Francisco began in 1883 and, in 1884, John L. Sullivan gave an exhibition boxing match. Chief Geronimo and other Indians were held prisoner at the Quadrangle at Fort Sam Houston in 1886.

In 1887, an artesian well was dug for the Crystal Ice Co. Oil was discovered on the George Dullnig Ranch (now Brooks Field).

The first mesquite block paving was laid on Alamo Plaza in 1889.

In 1895, Beethoven Hall was built and Theodore Roosevelt assembled the Rough Riders in 1898. In 1899, an ostrich farm located near San Pedro Springs sold ostrich plumes. The Hot Sulphur Wells Amusement Park opened in 1907.

In 1913, the river channel was changed at Bowen's Island. The Tower Life Building now stands approximately where the island was located. A concrete bridge on Navarro Street replaced the old steel mill bridge in 1922.

The Conservation Society was organized in 1924 and, in 1925, the City Water Works was purchased by the city from private owners through the sale of bonds.

In 1924, Municipal Auditorium, the city's World War I memorial, was completed. In 1926, both the Aztec and Texas theaters opened.

Winston Churchill visited San Antonio in 1927, and in 1928, the Milam Building opened as the first air conditioned office building in the world.

Randolph Air Force Base was opened in 1930. Nine years later, the restoration of La Villita and the San Antonio River beautification projects were started under the Work Projects Administration.[31]

THE NAT LEWIS MILL NEXT TO THE NAVARRO STREET BRIDGE.   *The Institute of Texan Cultures*

CHAPTER FOUR

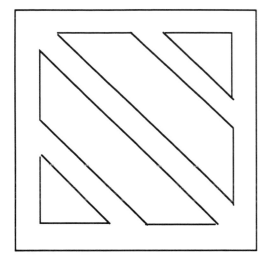

A Walk on the River In 1980

A few years ago, I was strolling along the San Antonio River Walk with my dog when I heard a visitor ask a most interesting question: "Who had the foresight to build such a beautiful River Walk?"

Several thoughts flashed through my mind as I continued to stroll. Not many local people are aware of how this River Walk was developed.

Ironically, visitors have to remind us of how we take some things for granted. The River Walk seen today emerged through the combined contributions of many people, although a single individual is most responsible for the concept of making such special and unusual use of a river in the middle of a downtown.

Creative thinking at its best, I thought — plants, trees, all coordinated to enhance shops, hotels, and sidewalk restaurants. As we strolled, I continued to muse about the visitor's question. My thoughts were interrupted by laughter from a group seated at one of the outdoor restaurants. At another table there was serious discussion about the economy. From one there came an inquiry about the name of the large trees towering high into the air.

A customer asked the waiter, "How long has this River Walk been this way?" The waiter shrugged and turned his attention to taking an order.

As my dog sniffed the aroma of mozzarella cheese wafting from an Italian restaurant, the visitor's question kept repeating in my mind, nagging my own curiosity.

As I paused by the Italian restaurant to admire the large cypress trees, a large barge full of people came by, the river travelers happily greeting strangers who were walking along or seated at the outdoor dining tables on both sides of the river.

For a moment, it seemed as if everyone sharing this day had forgotten all mundane problems and found relaxation along this River Walk winding through the heart of the city. I wondered whether someone had visualized how the river could turn downtown from a place usually avoided into a pleasant haven for millions of visitors from around the world.

My dog Sola glanced across the river to another restaurant from which came the distinct aroma of Mexican food. As we strolled by, mariachis were tuning their instruments for the next request.

Up we went over an arched bridge. On top of the bridge, I looked left and marveled at the stretch of river lined with plants, flowers, trees, and rock gardens leading to the Marriott Hotel and the Convention Center.

Sola strained at the leash as we moved under the Market Street Bridge. We strolled by an Irish pub and a group of tables at river level of the Hilton Palacio del Rio Hotel. Two people were sipping strawberry daiquiris just prepared by the barmaid at a small, attractively decorated sidewalk cart.

My thoughts returned to the planning and detailed work someone did in order to so thoroughly blend the history and natural beauty of this place.

ARCHED BRIDGES, RIVER BARGES AND LUSH GREENERY CREATE THE ROMANTIC SETTING HUGMAN PLANNED FOR THE RIVER WALK.
San Antonio Convention and Visitors Bureau

I remembered reading descriptions of the River Bend from the 1920's suggesting it was an unattractive, rat-infested area everyone largely ignored. How did this now-charming River Walk come to be?

The clinking of champagne glasses from a toast on a passing river barge provided a momentary musical interruption of my thoughts. About a dozen people were enjoying a meal being served as they slowly cruised down the river. Sola's surge on the leash was a reminder we were nearing a steak restaurant across from the Arneson River Theater.

Customers at this restaurant and a neighboring one were watching the stage area, eagerly anticipating the next performance. As we followed flagstone walks, then pebbled ones, we passed a refreshing waterfall, its constant splashes creating a relaxing tattoo along this area of the River Walk.

Sola moved very close to the rock retaining walls that protect the river bank from erosion. I noted that these walls form a sense of structure while enhancing the tranquility of the river. I also realized there is a delicate balance between commercial and park-like areas along the river. But what makes the River Walk different from just a surface street is that its design successfully tips the scale toward the beauty and peace of the river.

In such an atmosphere, one's thoughts and reflections can easily wander far from the realities of a troubled world that seems to have been left behind. We reached the floodgates by the Granada Apartments and quickly climbed the steps. As I paused, I glanced at the plain concrete flood by-pass in the main river channel, but a gentle pull on the leash reminded me we had not completed our walk.

We suddenly emerged onto the noisy, bustling streets of downtown San Antonio and quickly crossed through traffic on Commerce Street to descend to the River Walk again where our tempo slowed and returned to that of the gently moving water.

As I noticed an interesting array of patterns and designs on the walkways, the question I had earlier overheard once again jumped into my thoughts: "Who had the foresight to build such a beautiful River Walk?"

As I sat on a wooden bench between two large cypress trees, Sola snuggled next to me. The passengers in a barge reacted at seeing the warm rapport that was so obvious between a man and his dog. And I reflected on their sense of harmony that seemed so to reflect the peaceful mood of the River Walk.

Like millions of other people before and since, they had discovered a unique, enjoyable encounter with the beauty of nature right in the center of downtown in one of the largest cities in America.

As I stroked Sola's ears, I thought again of the visitor's question. It was a question I kept hearing in my mind whenever I strolled the River Walk.

Then, by marvelous coincidence, I found the answer to the visitor's indelible query in a most unusual way — by writing

VERNON ZUNKER, HIS WIFE, ROSALIE, AND THEIR DOGS PAUSE DURING A STROLL ALONG THE RIVER WALK SEVERAL YEARS AGO.
Photo by Daryl Engel

a book about the River Walk and about the person whose genius and foresight and dreams made it a reality.

In the fall of 1981, Mr. and Mrs. Frank W. Phelps expressed interest in publishing a book about the unheralded contribution of architect Robert H.H. Hugman to the creation of San Antonio's River Walk.

After learning of Hugman's original design concepts for the river and his devotion to realizing those plans, the Phelpses wanted to chronicle Hugman's achievements in a book. At their request, I agreed to write it.

Hugman had died about a year before the book project was launched. While I did not have the privilege of meeting him, my respect for him grew as I read his speeches and studied his architectural designs and learned of the struggle he waged.

Hugman's determination even outlasted the Depression that at first made his grand vision of the river seem an absurd fantasy. Ironically, in the end, it was the recovery effort from the Depression that provided the public funds needed to make Hugman's dream come true.

The most appropriate use of the San Antonio River has been on the minds of San Antonians for years.

An article written on August 23, 1887, in the San Antonio Daily Express made this rather remarkable observation:

"Our river can best serve the interests of the city and contribute to its welfare and happiness as that of a clear beautiful winding stream through its center. Such a stream, like a silver thread running under bridges, darting around curves and sparkling in the sunlight, would make up for much that is lacking in the improvement and adornment of our city.

"To the stranger, it would be a perfect treasure of delight and add day by day to the love our people bear the old town . . . its banks could be converted into flower beds, and pleasure boats (could) afford recreation . . . and our river would become the jewel of Texas."[32]

Remember, this vision of the San Antonio River was a dream first talked about in public in 1887.

What proved to be a most prophetic article seemed to set the stage for what would happen to the river in the next century, but only after a few disasters along the way.

FOR DECADES AFTER THE RIVER WALK WAS BUILT, IT REMAINED UNUSED AND ISOLATED FROM THE REST OF DOWNTOWN. THIS
YOUNG COUPLE STOPS FOR PRIVATE REFLECTIONS ON 'ROSITA'S BRIDGE' AT THE NOW-BUSY AND POPULAR ARNESON RIVER THEATER.
San Antonio Express-News Photo

CHAPTER FIVE

The Shops of Aragon And Romula

The story of the development of the San Antonio River Walk begins with a disastrous flood.

In September of 1921, the San Antonio River overflowed its banks from the drainage of heavy rains and swept through downtown. The flood waters were eight to nine feet deep on Houston Street. More than 50 people lost their lives and there was extensive property damage.

Outraged citizens demanded that officials take steps to control the devastating floodwaters. Many looked upon the river as a detriment to the city's development. City government was forced to take action.

An engineering firm was contracted by the city to provide specific recommendations for solving the problem. Included were the building of Olmos Dam to hold back heavy rain run-off and then gradually release it, the straightening and widening of the river at certain locations, construction of a concrete flood water channel from Seventh Street (now Brooklyn Avenue) to Nueva Street, and, yes, filling in the area of the river known today as the River Walk and making it into a street.

There was no opposition to the idea of building Olmos Dam, which was constructed in 1927, or to widening and straightening some areas of the river to better handle flood waters.

But major controversy erupted when news reached civic groups about the proposal to pour concrete floors in certain sections of the river and to convert the horseshoe-shaped River Bend area into a drainage culvert covered over with pavement.

The City Federation of Women's Clubs and the San Antonio Conservation Society led the fight to save the River Bend area and to preserve the natural river channel. These groups made it clear that any straightening of their "lovely winding San Antonio River" should only be done as needed to control floodwaters. A puppet show entitled "The Goose that Laid the Golden Egg" written by Miss Emily Edwards, was presented to city commissioners by Conservation Society members to dramatize their stance in favor of maintaining the River Bend and opposition to any plan to pave the river over and turn it into a storm drain and a street.

They also strongly objected to anything that would detract from the river's natural flow. And, finally, it was suggested that the river banks be converted into a city park.

That same river park concept was also the dream of a young architect, Robert H.H. Hugman, who had returned to his native San Antonio in 1927 after spending three years in New Orleans. Hugman had been very impressed with the conservation movement he witnessed there.

The preservation of Old World charm, beauty, local color, and the character of the Vieux Carre district in New Orleans had greatly influenced his professional interests. The timing of his return to San Antonio and his recent experiences in New Orleans was a fortunate coincidence and helped inspire concepts that evolved into his comprehensive plan for preserving and enhancing the downtown San Antonio River channel.

WATER IN THE RIVER BEND DROPS TO STREET LEVEL AT THE ST. MARY'S STREET BRIDGE DURING THE DEVASTATING 1921 FLOOD.

RIVER LEVEL OF THE PETROLEUM COMMERCE BUILDING, LEFT, IS INUNDATED. HIGH WATER MARKS ARE VISIBLE ON WINDOW PIERS.
The Institute of Texan Cultures

Hugman shared his ideas with Mrs. Lane Taylor, then president of the San Antonio Conservation Society. She persuaded city officials to attend a meeting where there would be a presentation and discussion of a plan to beautify the river.

The dramatic stage setting for this forum had evolved from the controversy surrounding the river. The meeting was announced and action setting the whole future course of the San Antonio River got under way.[33]

On Friday, June 28, 1929, Mayor Chambers and two city commissioners met with a group of property owners and other civic leaders to hear the young architect describe his plans for beautifying the San Antonio River.

One can only speculate that some of those in attendance were interested in a feasible plan for the river's development. But the overriding question for most at the meeting probably was: "What do you do with a river that flows through downtown and has caused havoc with its flash floods?"

Although tamed to a considerable degree by then, the river was still a problem, its banks were littered and its water was sometimes foul. Hidden from view and used as a backyard by many, the river was regarded as an undesirable element in the neighborhood. Deteriorating buildings along the river banks were reminders of the prevalence of this negative attitude. Meanwhile, several organizations such as the Conservation Society advocated preserving the river's natural beauty. Buttressed by a shared desire for finding overall solutions to the river's future, the group gathered.[34]

To ask how many individuals over the years had dreamed of enhancing the river's beauty and discovering its hidden opportunities is a moot question. But to claim that only one ever had such a dream would, in effect, do the river an injustice. Surely, many dreamed of elaborate schemes of what could be done to enhance the river's charm. For one man, the necessary link in making his dream a reality took place on that warm day in June, 1929.

Hugman's speech with the intriguing title, "The Shops of Aragon and Romula," opened with his observation that San Antonio had doubled in population during the previous decade of 1919-1929 and had been transformed from "a sleepy Southern town to a future metropolis."

He then made his first reference to the central theme of his speech by noting, "the historic tradition and natural beauty (of the river) must be sacredly preserved if we would build the right foundation for steady growth and future interest."

Hugman's interest in maintaining the historical and unique character of the river was a singular theme emphasized repeatedly throughout his speech.

Those reflections on the San Antonio River would be repeated by Hugman many times during the next 35 to 40 years.

He told the crowd how he conceived of his plan.

"I was sitting at my studio window. The slanting rays of the late afternoon sun cast long shadows on the cypress-lined

After the 1921 floods left nine feet of San Antonio River water in downtown, boats were pressed into use as street transportation, as seen here at the intersection of St. Mary's and Travis streets. *The Institute of Texan Cultures*

Jumble of wreckage clogs the Navarro Street Bridge as water from the 1921 flood recedes below deck level, as seen in lower left corner, leaving behind trolley rails and ties, house shutters, garden lattice, furniture and other debris. *The Institute of Texan Cultures*

AS A BOY, ROBERT HUGMAN PLAYED AND FISHED ALONG THE SAN ANTONIO RIVER. YOUNG HUGMAN, CENTER, AND HIS FRIENDS STRIKE A DASHING POSE BY A CAR. IN HIS PORTRAIT AS A DESIGN PROFESSIONAL, HUGMAN SPORTS A MOUSTACHE AND A PIPE.
Photos from Anne Hugman Robinson

banks of the river, when in my meditation there came to me a vision — at first a vague, uncertain dream. But it has been mulling through my mind for many a day since the first thought came to me and has been crystallized into something real and tangible. We read descriptions of the old cities in Spain, of a narrow, winding street barred to vehicular traffic, yet holding the best shops, clubs, banks, and cafes; prosperous, yet alluring with its shadowed doorways and quaint atmosphere — a street far removed from our modern business thoroughfare. And when we read, we longed to go to see and enjoy (it). So, it occurred to me that such a street in the very heart of our growing city would do much to enhance its interest and naught to impair its progress."

Hugman continued his presentation by outlining his ideas for what he called "The Shops of Aragon."

He suggested a narrow cobblestone street be constructed on the river bank behind businesses facing Houston, Soledad, Commerce, and St.Mary's streets. His plan called for construction of small shops, apartments, cafes, cabarets, and dance clubs along this street of his imagination.

Hugman also endorsed the construction of a section of the controversial project known as the "channel by-pass cutoff" between Houston and Commerce Streets where the river turns east to begin its loop through the central city. He recommended that a heavy steel flood gate be placed at the north end of the channel to regulate the flow of water through the River Bend. Smaller dams down river would regulate water flow through the channel cutoff.

Romula was to be accessed from the Shops of Aragon by a footbridge across the channel near Commerce Street that Hugman envisioned as "no more than an interesting flagstone walk along the river bank." Hugman proposed that shops and restaurants be developed on both sides of the river between Crockett and Commerce streets. He accurately predicted the future of the Paseo del Rio, saying it presented "an opportunity for unlimited development of beauty and interest."

Hugman's next vision was of river boats fashioned after the gondolas of Venice:

"Imagine this boat ride down the river on a balmy night, fanned by a gentle breeze carrying the delightful aroma of honeysuckle and sweet olive, old-fashioned street lamps casting fantastic shadows on the surface of the water, strains of soft music in the air; all of this would be the night life of Romula."

At this point, Hugman stressed that what he had presented was largely aesthetic. He also recognized that the Shops of Aragon and Romula must have commercial appeal to realize their development.

"Unless there was a practical side, the entire scheme would be quickly relegated to the annals of other fanciful imaginings and promptly forgotten. It is not mere idealism, and we will reflect in a moment on its commercial aspect."

HUGMAN ENVISIONED RIVER SHOPS ALONG THE EAST BANK OF THE RIVER FROM CROCKETT STREET, LEFT, TO COMMERCE STREET, RIGHT.

THE WEST SIDE OF THE RIVER WALK FROM COMMERCE STREET, LEFT, TO CROCKETT PROPOSED SEVERAL INTERNATIONAL RESTAURANTS.

SKETCH OF A SPANISH-STYLE 'PLAZITA' WAS PART OF HUGMAN'S VISION OF OLD WORLD CHARM TO TRANSFORM THE RIVER WALK.
Photo from Frank W. Phelps

Many of Hugman's dreams have become reality. Although the Shops of Aragon he envisioned were never built, the River Bend area has developed remarkably as Hugman imagined, with flagstone walks, plants, shops, cafes, night clubs, apartments and hotels.

The romantic Old World eclectic architecture and unique forms of entertainment he envisioned are very recognizable elements along the Paseo del Rio of today.

Hugman once explained to his granddaughter-in-law that the name of his Shops of Aragon and Romula had been borrowed from Spanish Majorca, a part of the Balearic Islands in the Mediterranean Sea some 130 miles south of Barcelona.

Daryl Engel, a former urban planner for the City of San Antonio, recalled from a visit there some of the charm of the City of Palma.

"There are many areas in the city where shoppers can stroll without concern for vehicle traffic. I remember places like Palma and other towns along the Spanish Mediterranean. They were phenomenal. What is important is the street walls along the winding pedestrian streets create small canyons — spatial definition — which usually do not exist in American cities. The facade scale, detail, and color create conducive environments for human activity in public spaces," Engel said.

Perhaps Hugman had read descriptions of Majorca's largest city, Palma, and was impressed with the shopping areas zoned only for pedestrians. Palma, being well- known for its colorful shops along narrow winding promenades, may have been the model for Hugman's Shops of Aragon.

Romula, the name originally given the River Bend area, was chosen because, as Hugman put it, "the sound was romantic."

Perhaps Romula was Hugman's way of subtly linking the Paseo del Rio with the exotic as a way of drawing attention to the unique opportunity that development of the river presented to San Antonio and its citizens. His dream was to create a unique atmosphere through landscaping and architectural elements drawn from San Antonio's historic past.

Hugman's quote in the San Antonio Light of February, 24, 1972, underscores this point:

"Paseo del Rio's success will always lie in the unique, aesthetic and romantic appeal experienced by people who visit and wish to share it with others, be it pictures, or another visit."

During one of Hugman's conversations with his daughter, Anne, he told her that the name given his plan was part of his total concept for the river's development. He saw that development as a privilege of foresight, a vantage point he had acquired concerning the river's potential in San Antonio's future, and the name chosen for the plan aesthetically reinforced his whole idea. The development of this concept, he confided, was what he considered his major purpose in life.[35]

The Shops of Aragon and Romula were, indeed, seminal plans. Hugman hoped that his idea would have a major impact on the beautification of the San Antonio River and help guide its future development.

In 1929, he emphasized that his design scheme must "be treated as a whole, and not as separate units."

Thus, he suggests that development of the river follow a master plan with the flexibility to nurture not only commercial development, but also the natural beauty of the river with spaces reserved for plant life and peaceful areas for quiet reflection.

One of Hugman's most important points was the need to achieve balance in the developmental process. In essence, his plan would enhance and maintain the natural setting of the river while commercial development evolved.

His message is especially relevant to those today who see only the tremendous commercial opportunities the river offers.

According to Hugman, the river must keep its original character while protecting the spaces that express its different moods if it is to remain a viable part of what makes San Antonio unique. Preserving the charm, history and Old World atmosphere of the river was an underlying theme of Hugman's aesthetically oriented schema of the Shops of Aragon and Romula.[36]

SHOPS OF ARAGON AND ROMULA · BY·R·H·H·HUGMAN ARCHITECT

1929 · SAN·ANTONIO · 1929

THIS IS THE COVER PAGE OF THE LEATHER-BOUND BOOK HUGMAN PREPARED TO PRESENT HIS RIVER WALK DEVELOPMENT PLAN.
Photo from Frank W. Phelps

CHAPTER SIX

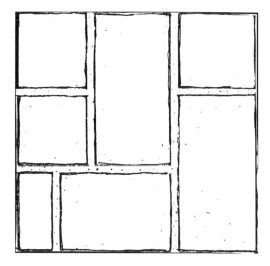

The Vision in Hugman's Own Words

The following is the text of the speech delivered by Robert H.H. Hugman in 1929:

FOREWORD

San Antonio, in the past few years, has seen a great awakening. Its population has doubled in 10 years. So phenomenal has been the change from a sleepy southern town to a coming metropolis, that the rhythmic sound of its steel hammers and buzzing of its new factories, is echoing far and wide, causing a mighty nation to pause and wonder and applaud.

But while we look with joy and satisfaction on this great commercial development, we must not forget that San Antonio is the "Winter Playground of America" and its historic traditions and natural beauty must be sacredly preserved if we would build the right foundation for steady growth and future interest.

In all of our great America, we cannot find another city with history quite so laden with interest. The blood-stained Alamo, the old cathedral and the missions with their incomparable beauty lend to our city a poignant charm.

All of these are properly appreciated, but there is one great asset of San Antonio that is not being capitalized upon — its beautiful winding river.

I was sitting at my studio window. The slanting rays of a late afternoon sun cast long shadows on the cypress lined banks of the river, when, in my meditation, there came to me a vision — at first, a vague, uncertain dream. But it has been mulling through my mind for many a day since the first thought came to me and has been crystallized into something real and tangible.

We read descriptions of the old cities in Spain, of a narrow, winding street barred to vehicular traffic yet holding the best shops, clubs, banks and cafes; prosperous, yet alluring, with its shadowed doorways and quaint atmosphere. A street far removed from our modern business thoroughfare -- and when we read, we long to go to see and enjoy (it).

So, it occurred to me that such a street in the very heart of our growing city would do much to enhance its interest and naught to impair its progress.

ARAGON

Wedged in behind the pretentious business houses on Houston, Soledad, Commerce and St. Mary's, why not a quaint, old cobble-stoned street rambling lazily along the river? A street with Old World appeal. Small shops, a studio apartment where the artist or musician could both live and work, a small but very exclusive bachelor apartment, a cafe, cabaret and dance club would all do a thriving business in this atmosphere.

On this little street of my imagination, the shops would be built of old stone and brick of very simple architecture creating maximum charm at a minimum expense. They would be on the west side of the river between Houston Street and the

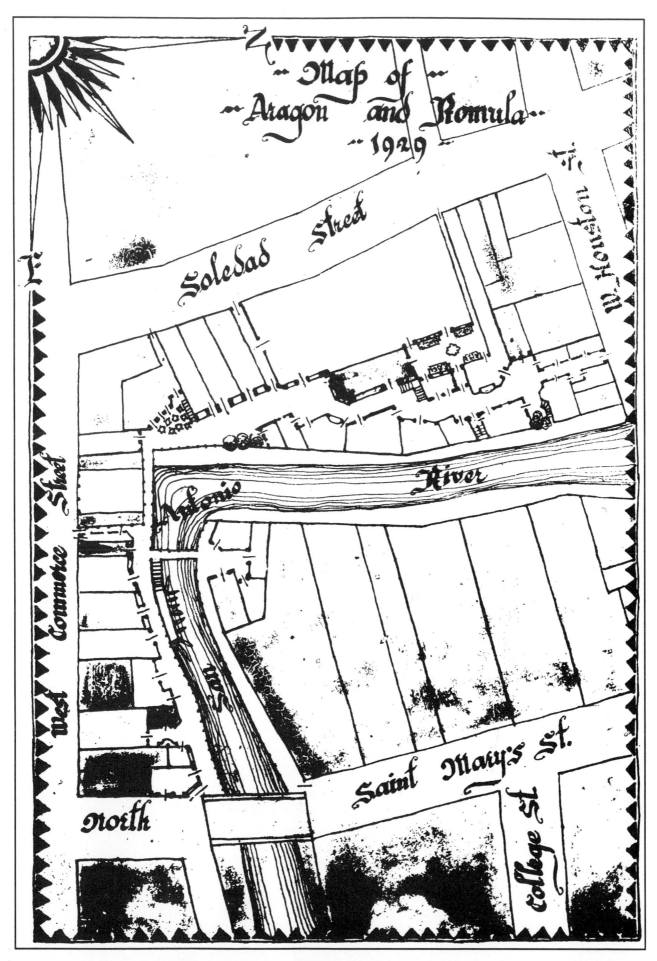

AS PART OF HIS ORIGINAL 1929 PRESENTATION, HUGMAN PREPARED THIS MAP OF HIS SHOPS OF ARAGON AND ROMULA ALONG THE RIVER BEHIND STORES ON SOLEDAD AND COMMERCE STREETS.   *Photo from Frank W. Phelps*

new channel at Commerce and would be called "The Shops of Aragon."

Then, near the entrance would be a little court called the "Court of Roses," a typical old Spanish patio, gay with flowers and fresh with running water. At the other end of the street would be a "plazita" directly in front of the cafe and used by it for the outdoor table service.

ROMULA

Upon leaving Aragon with its shadowed charm, we come to a footbridge which crosses the new channel in one graceful span, bringing us to Romula, which in pleasing contrast, is a tiny little street sparkling with sunshine. In fact, it is no more than an interesting flagstone walk along the river bank with shops similar to those of Aragon on the one side — both banks of the river being treated in like manner.

Beginning at the new channel, Romula would follow the river's meanderings around the Horseshoe Bend to the Plaza Hotel, presenting an opportunity for unlimited development of beauty and interest.

At the far end of the street of Romula — between Presa and St. Mary's Streets by the Plaza Hotel where the banks are unusually wide — the river could be divided into two smaller streams to wind through a sunken garden of loveliness to compare with the famous Gardens of the Alcazar or the Alhambra.

A fitting climax to the whole scheme will be gaily colored boats fashioned after the gondolas of Venice, though of Spanish design, to take pleasure seekers over the picturesque route from Travis Street to the Plaza Hotel. The public would welcome this unique form of entertainment, and its romantic appeal would insure its popularity.

Imagine this boat ride down the river on a balmy night, fanned by a gentle breeze carrying the delightful aroma of honeysuckle and sweet olive, old-fashioned street lamps casting fantastic shadows on the surface of the water, strains of soft music in the air, all of this would be the night life of Romula.

SUMMARY

In the foregoing presentation of the Shops of Aragon and Romula, the appeal has been largely aesthetic, and unless there was a practical side, the entire scheme would be quickly relegated to the annals of other fanciful imaginings and promptly forgotten. It is not mere idealism, and we will reflect a moment on its commercial aspect.

The river is sometimes looked upon with disfavor, as taking too much room in its vagabondish winding through the valuable downtown area. This, I believe, is an entirely wrong slant on the situation.

To me, the river is one of nature's greatest gifts to San Antonio and should be appreciated and developed as such. Our city is the mecca for thousands of tourists each year, not only

OUTDOOR DINING ALONG THE RIVER WALK UNDER TOWERING TREES AND AMID ARCHED BRIDGES AND OTHER ROMANTIC TOUCHES ARE THE SPECTACULAR DESIGN LEGACY OF ARCHITECT ROBERT HUGMAN. *San Antonio Convention and Visitors Bureau*

because of its wonderful climate, but because of its "atmosphere." The spirit of the past lives in its famous Alamo, old cathedral, missions and quaint plazas. These are things that set San Antonio apart. This river project would add beauty to our thriving business center and would provide a pleasant shortcut from Houston Street to the rapidly developing part of Commerce Street and would, in no way, interfere with flood prevention measures.

Think what a wealth of advertising material the city would have in the Shops of Aragon and Romula, lending themselves, as they would, to the most colorful descriptions.

The advantages to the property owners are obvious, as the scheme will give them at least two fronts — and, in some cases, as many as five — while the lure of the unusual will draw throngs of people to their shops. But, it is not the property owners alone who will profit; it is a civic improvement that means an even greater San Antonio and must, consequently, rebound to the ultimate good of all its citizens.

In conclusion, if you find yourselves in accord with this idea and believe it feasible and worthy of execution, then I will appreciate having your autograph on the signature page.

FRATERNITY

To the property owners along the river: I have presented to you the Shops of Aragon and Romula, endorsed by the mayor, city commissioners, flood prevention engineers and many other prominent citizens who have the welfare of San Antonio at heart. I realize, of course, that in the final analysis, the success or failure of the project depends upon your reception of it.

The idea is absolutely original and I have spent a great deal of time in preparing it for presentation. I know that I am giving you a plan that will mean much to you from a monetary standpoint, if it is handled properly. Like a stage setting, designed and directed by one mind to produce the proper unity of thought and feeling; so must this scheme be treated as a whole, and not as separate units.

The shops, lighting effects, advertising — everything — must be designed to create the right "atmosphere." To do this, it will be necessary that we unite our interests.

Will you work with me to this end?

A BY-PASS CHANNEL TO DIVERT STORM RUNOFF PAST DOWNTOWN WAS BUILT BEFORE THE RIVER WALK IMPROVEMENTS PROJECT. THIS WATER-SPOTTED PHOTO OF DEMOLITION AND CONSTRUCTION NORTH OF VILLITA STREET, BOTTOM, ALSO SHOWS THE MARKET STREET AND COMMERCE STREET BRIDGES AND, IN THE DISTANCE, THE MILAM BUILDING. *The Institute of Texan Cultures*

CHAPTER SEVEN

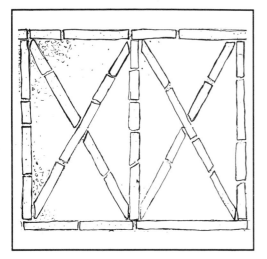

The Construction Of the River Walk

Transforming parts of the San Antonio River into the Shops of Aragon and Romula required considerable effort beyond developing a vision of how it should look. While Hugman's ideas received positive reactions from numerous organizations in the early 1930's, the Depression made funding a river beautification project difficult.

But Hugman did not give up. He continued his efforts to promote the San Antonio River as a viable part of the city's future development. He spent six years speaking to civic groups and calling on businessmen like a door-to-door salesman promoting the river beautification plan.

Hugman was quoted in an article in the San Antonio Light on October 15, 1930: "I was born and raised in San Antonio, and my interest in the flood prevention program is the natural outgrowth of the love of the river that had its inception when as a boy I fished along its banks. I'm sure that most of us share this sentiment."

His October 11, 1935, talk to the local chapter of the Daughters of the American Revolution was covered by the San Antonio Express and included this observation:

"We have a priceless beauty spot in our river and could easily make it so that homes and even business places would be remodeled to face the river instead of turning their back doors to it. The plan drawn up proposes to build stairways down to the river bank in the downtown section, and to place benches there for the use of the public. The natural beauty could be enhanced by planting flowers and shrubbery."

An article in the March 11, 1939, San Antonio Express has Hugman describing his proposed river theater as "a small intimate theater seating about 1,000 spectators. The purpose is to produce the miracle plays traditional to the Spanish southwest and other native drama. The enterprise will not be commercial, but cultural -- an effort to catch and express the true spirit of San Antonio."

Hugman repeatedly acknowledged the leadership of the San Antonio Conservation Society in the development of the river. He credited the members with convincing the city to maintain the natural beauty of the river. He said they had been of inestimable value in the 1920's and often noted that their continued active interest in the development of the river was a great source of support for him.

Several other civic groups joined the battle. On October 18, 1929, the City Federation of Women's Clubs presented to Mayor Chambers and the city commissioners a resolution urging that the city hire Hugman to design the river beautification project.

In the spring of 1938, Hugman's concept won endorsements from the San Antonio Advertising Club and the Real Estate Board.[37,38]

RIVER FLOOD IMPROVEMENTS INCLUDED THIS WORK TO STRAIGHTEN A BEND IN THE CHANNEL NEAR THE MUNICIPAL AUDITORIUM.
The Institute of Texan Cultures

HOTEL ENTREPRENEUR AND LATER SAN ANTONIO MAYOR, JACK WHITE, CENTER, WAS AN EARLY INFLUENTIAL SUPPORTER OF HUGMAN'S RIVER WALK DESIGNS, BUT BECAME A KEY FIGURE IN HUGMAN'S FIRING.   *Photo from Robert H. Turk*

WORK BEGINS ON THE FLOODGATE AND WATERFALLS NEAR THE BEXAR COUNTY COURTHOUSE. THE GRACEFUL HORSESHOE FALLS AND GATE BY THE GRANADA APARTMENTS KEPT WATER IN THE RIVER WALK LEVEL, YET FLOWING. *Photo from Robert H. Turk*

A CURVING STAIRWAY IS BEING BUILT DOWN TO THE RIVER WALK NEXT TO THE SMITH-YOUNG TOWER, NOW THE TOWER LIFE BUILDING. BEYOND AT RIGHT IS WHAT TODAY SERVES AS THE CITY PUBLIC SERVICE HEADQUARTERS.   *Photo from Robert H. Turk*

RIVER WALK CONSTRUCTION IS UNDER WAY SOUTH OF THE COMMERCE STREET BRIDGE. THE CASA RIO RESTAURANT SITE IS ON THE LEFT BANK. IN THE DISTANCE IS THE HOTEL HAMILTON, NOW THE LOSOYA BUILDING. *Photo from Robert H. Turk*

Jack White, a hotel entrepreneur and later mayor of San Antonio, endorsed Hugman's river improvement plan in 1935 and enthusiastically supported it in public. His persistence took him before many civic groups and he convinced a number of owners of downtown river frontage property to pledge $2.50 per square foot to finance the beautification work. He also helped organize a river beautification board.

Early in 1938, Mayor C.K. Quin and the City Commission rejected river plans submitted by the beautification board because city officials had agreed not to fund new projects and to try to reduce the city budget because of the Depression.[39,40]

Jack White continued fighting for the river plan and recruited support from yet another group, Improvement District 15, which had been created by the city in mid-April of 1938. The group consisted of owners who had property along and residents who lived on either side of the river from Fourth Street (now Lexington) to Villita Street.[41]

Finally, all the private discussions, public speeches, endorsements, luncheons, meetings and talks paid off.

On October 25, a special referendum on an assessment of 1.5 cents per $100 assessed valuation was approved by the improvement district's voters.

The vote on the San Antonio River improvements proved to be another of those legendary events in a state where stories flourish about dead voters deciding crucial party primaries and even general elections by listing cemetery addresses on official voting records.

Voting on the river bond issue was restricted to "property owners" living in the district established in the vicinity of the downtown River Bend. When supporters of the river plan discovered early on that two of the five property owners in the district opposed the bond issue, officials suddenly declared that guests staying at the Plaza Hotel were qualified to vote.

They had found a legal loophole. It didn't specify that eligible voters must live in the district and own "real property," meaning land or buildings. So, since Plaza Hotel guests were "living" in the district, they were declared eligible to vote if they had any "property" with them, even such personal items as small as a watch, just so they owned the "property."

The bond issue passed 74 to 2.

The vote approved $75,000 in city funds needed to secure a $355,000 federal grant through the Work Projects Administration (WPA).[42]

Jack White, as chairman of the river beautification board, worked tirelessly as a liaison between city government and the WPA.

On October 30, 1938, he was quoted in The San Antonio Light as follows: "San Antonio has not begun to realize all its

To allow workers to build support walls, sidewalks and other River Walk amenities, the water was diverted first to one side of the river channel, then to the other. Fortunately, no floods interrupted the construction progress.
Photo from Robert H. Turk

YEARS BEFORE THE RIVER WALK BEAUTIFICATION PROJECT WAS CARRIED OUT, HUGMAN ENDORSED THE MAIN CHANNEL BY-PASS BUILT TO DIVERT HIGH WATER PAST, RATHER THAN THROUGH, THE RIVER BEND AREA.   *San Antonio Express-News Photo*

possibilities as a tourist resort. The river beautification project will make San Antonio unique among cities of the country, as I know of no other city with a beautiful river winding through its downtown section. The committee is confident that when the beautification plan becomes a reality, tourists will come from all over the world to see this unusual attraction and to experience a ride in gondolas through downtown San Antonio."[43,44]

The influence of Hugman's Shops of Aragon and Romula on Jack White's perspective of the San Antonio River is quite evident. But White's own creativity and foresight are reflected in his recognition of the uniqueness of the San Antonio River Walk and his prediction of its universal popularity.

On December 16, 1938, Hugman was hired as architect of the San Antonio River beautification project at a fee of 2.5 per cent of the total cost of the project, but not to exceed $6,600.

A few months shy of the tenth anniversary of his presentation to Mayor Chambers, Hugman's dream of beautifying the river was about to come true. Meantime, the theme of his concept appeared frequently over the years in newspaper columns and was often a discussion topic for civic groups. Subjects such as riverside businesses and shops, outdoor cafes, tropical growth along the river, and gondola rides were "in" topics.[45]

Ernie Pyle, the well-known columnist, was invited to San Antonio in 1939 to see the river plan and the progress of its construction.

He wrote that the San Antonio River project was an American Venice of the future. His article both rewarded and encouraged those who had worked so hard for the river project.

The New York Times published an article on February 12, 1939, describing the development of the San Antonio River as a "Venice of America" and "Gondolas for Texas." Hugman's concept of what to do with a river in a downtown area had been recognized. Soon, after all the money was authorized by the city and WPA, Robert Turk was selected superintendent of construction.

Turk, a native Texan, arrived in San Antonio in 1917 by covered wagon from Big Spring. His father had obtained a carpenter's job near San Antonio and sent word to his family to sell the stock, ship the furniture by rail and bring other belongings in the wagon. After 17 days, Turk arrived with his family, two horses, two mules and a riding horse.

Turk knew the meaning of work and soon after graduation from San Antonio Technical School, he bought a set of carpenter's tools, noting "this decision I never regretted."

Turk and Hugman met shortly after Turk got his job as superintendent early in 1939. From their first meeting on, they were the best of friends. The two conferred practically every day as they strolled along the river bank.

RIVER WALK CONSTRUCTION SUPERINTENDENT ROBERT H. TURK, FOREGROUND, PAUSES FOR A MOMENT WITH SOME OF HIS CREW AS BEAUTIFICATION WORK BEGINS IN 1939. TURK AND HUGMAN BECAME CLOSE FRIENDS DURING THE TWO-YEAR BUILDING PROJECT.
Photo from Robert H. Turk

WORKMEN CONSTRUCT FORMS FOR THE POURED CONCRETE STAIRWAY CONNECTING NAVARRO STREET TO THE RIVER WALK. MOST OF HUGMAN'S STAIRWELLS REVEALED A FLAIR FOR FORMAL BAROQUE SHAPES THAT WERE FINISHED IN NATURAL-CUT STONE TRIM.
Photo from Robert H. Turk

THE NORTH FLOOD GATE THAT ISOLATES THE RIVER BEND FROM THE FLOOD BY-PASS CHANNEL REFLECTS HUGMAN'S CONCERN FOR DESIGN DETAIL, AS EVEN THIS UTILITARIAN STRUCTURE HAS ROMANTIC SPANISH ARCHES AND AN ARBOR/COLONNADE AT THE TOP.
San Antonio Express-News Photo

Turk recalls the decisions they reached. "We would supervise the work on the river together. Hugman would tell us how and what he wanted and the rest of us would put it together for him."

In describing Hugman, Turk portrayed a dedicated man whose main goal in his early life seemed to be the beautification of the San Antonio River.

"He (Hugman) was way ahead of his time. Most people didn't understand what he was trying to do. I guess none of us realized the potential of the River Walk."

During construction of the River Walk, Turk supervised approximately 1000 men. He insisted that the stone masons should be given full credit for their contributions.

"They seemed to have a knack of knowing which rock to put where. When we would give a rock to a brick layer, he would chip around on it and get nowhere. But the stone masons got the job done!"

He explained that some of the workers would loaf on the job, but when he suggested that they were to work for Manuel, a tough foreman, they got to work. Manuel and others like him kept the project moving and were of inestimable value as members of a work force often forgotten for its contribution to the river's beauty.

A very important part of the project was the cleaning and deepening of the channel. Most of this work had to be done with shovels and wheelbarrows; a difficult, dirty and tedious task. At some locations, they could use a dragline, a crane with a specially designed bucket for excavation work.

Near Travis Street by the Texas Theater, the dragline hit a soft pocket, causing it to flip over and sink into the mud. Attempts to extricate it provided great amusement for the many sidewalk superintendents who were ever present during the construction.[46]

Many items were found in the drained river bed. Besides car frames, bicycle parts and bed springs, they found cannon balls, buggy beds, wagon wheels, pistols, ax heads and rotted cedar posts.

Of particular interest were the crayfish found in the cracks of old rock walls. They were said to be very delicious and were about the size of small lobsters currently served in restaurants.

A major effort was made to preserve the trees which lined the river. During the beautification, cypress trees taken from the banks of the Guadalupe River were planted near existing ones.

Many shrubs and small trees were removed and stored. Fig trees that were supposedly planted along the river by the Canary Islanders were carefully guarded and preserved.

When the river was drained, exposed roots were covered and regularly watered. Arboreal crutches were constructed

THE NORTH PRESA STREET BRIDGE AS IT LOOKED BEFORE RIVER WALK CONSTRUCTION BEGAN. IN THE DISTANCE, AT LEFT CENTER, IS THE SOUTH TEXAS BUILDING AT HOUSTON AND NAVARRO. TODAY, THE HYATT REGENCY HOTEL IS TO THE RIGHT OF THE BRIDGE.
The Institute of Texan Cultures

LOOKING SOUTH UNDER THE PRESA STREET BRIDGE AFTER HUGMAN'S 'FLOATING SIDEWALK,' RIGHT, WAS COMPLETED. TODAY, THE PASEO DEL ALAMO WATERWAY FLOWING THROUGH THE HYATT REGENCY HOTEL ATRIUM ENTERS THE RIVER AT THE LEFT IN THIS SCENE.
The Institute of Texan Cultures

for several trees along the river bank. Surgery was performed on many.

Approximately 11,734 trees and shrubs were added by the city, including 1,500 banana trees, along with 1,489 square yards of carpet grass. Garden clubs also donated plants.[47]

But not all was going well with the river beautification project. Conflicts between Hugman and city officials led to his dismissal on March 19, 1940.

According to an article in the San Antonio Light on the day of his firing, Hugman was fired for failing to hire a landscape architect and to supply certain plans as had been agreed upon earlier.

Ironically, Jack White approved Hugman's ouster, charging that Hugman had agreed to, but did not follow through with, employing a landscape architect at his own expense, and he said many of Hugman's cost estimates were erroneous.

Hugman said in the San Antonio Light on March 22, 1940, that the reason he was fired was because he refused to hire a landscape architect "who is close to Mayor Maverick politically."

He also told the Light:

"My discharge from the river improvement project was a specimen of machine politics which the present city administration had been playing with this and other city projects."

Hugman provided more details about his dismissal 31 years later in a memo presented to the Paseo del Rio Association on February 9, 1971:

"I was not fired for any of the reasons given in the newspapers at the time, but because the WPA project bookkeepers gave me proof of malpractices — the delivery of materials originally ordered for the river project went instead to the La Villita restoration project, which was also under construction.

"I presented photostatic copies of the materials and vouchers and other facts to Judge Claude V. Birkhead, a member of the river board and of one of the largest legal firms in the city. He expressed his ire by sending a message to Jack White calling for a meeting of the river board, which I was not allowed to attend.

"You guessed it — I got fired without a hearing, and not one member of the river board stood up for me, nor did anyone else, except WPA project personnel. This complete injustice hurt me personally, professionally and financially, and I was advised that I had little or no defense."

In late March 1940, Robert Hugman dejectedly gave up the plans for beautifying the San Antonio River to another architect, J. Fred Buenz.

"Hugman never really got over being fired," said Turk. "We would fish together after we both retired, and he talked about it many times. He felt somewhat better when he was honored

STONE CRUTCHES HELP SUPPORT TREES LEANING OVER THE RIVER WALK AND THE WATER. UNDER HUGMAN'S DETAILED LANDSCAPE PLAN, SOME TREES REQUIRED SURGERY, BUT MANY WERE RELOCATED TO BRACKENRIDGE PARK UNTIL THE SITE WORK WAS COMPLETED.

Photo from Robert H. Turk

THE CURVING STONE STAIRWAY ON THE NORTH BANK OF THE SOUTH PRESA STREET BRIDGE NEXT TO THE CARNEGIE LIBRARY, NOW THE HERTZBERG CIRCUS MUSEUM, WAS AMONG DOZENS OF STAIRS HUGMAN DESIGNED INTO HIS 2.5 MILES OF RIVER WALK IMPROVEMENTS.
Photo from Robert H. Turk

HUGMAN INCLUDED MANY CEDAR BENCHES AND OTHER FIXTURES AS PART OF HIS DESIGN THEME OF USING MATERIALS NATIVE TO THE SAN ANTONIO AREA. THESE CEDAR STEPS ACROSS FROM THE CASINO CLUB LEADING DOWN FROM THE CROCKETT STREET BRIDGE AND NEXT TO THE PRESA STREET BRIDGE HAVE BEEN REPLACED BY STONE STAIRS AND METAL RAILINGS FOR SAFETY AND EASIER MAINTENANCE.
Photo from Robert H. Turk

at the Arneson River Theater in 1978 and efforts were made to recognize his original work."

On March 14, 1941, the WPA river beautification project came to an end. The total cost of the project was $430,000, of which $75,000 was provided by the city bond issue.

The area improved included 21 blocks, totaling 8,500 feet of river bank from the South St. Mary's Street bridge by the Tower Life Building to the Fourth Street — now Lexington Street — bridge near the Municipal Auditorium.

It took 11,000 cubic yards of masonry and 3,200 yards of concrete to build the 17,000 feet of River Walk sidewalks. Also constructed were 31 stairways — 30 in rock and one of split cedar posts — leading to the river bank from 21 bridges. Numerous benches made of stone, cement and cedar were placed in strategic locations along the river.[48]

At the completion of the WPA project, Mayor Maury Maverick, who was instrumental in obtaining the project funds, submitted a report that said, in part:

"The large cities of America were not planned. Men built haphazardly, wherever they found what seemed at the moment to be suitable places. The result was ugly factory districts and crowded and unsanitary residential sections which too often became hideous, unlivable breeding places of crime, sickness and unhappiness.

"Rivers within the city have been left alone to become dirty canals, their banks occupied by the ugliest types of commerce or by buildings that are unfit for human habitation. Their original beauty has been lost. Only planning can restore it.

"The River Beautification Project is not a complete plan for San Antonio. It is, however, an important part of a plan to make the city more beautiful and more livable. We believe that in all the United States of America there is no city in which a river has been made a more atttactive resort for all the people."[49]

Hugman had essentially expressed most of these thoughts during the late 1920's. But the concept architect would have to wait for more than two decades to be recognized when he was no longer in an official position to maintain and promote the river beautification program.

During the next 15 years, the River Walk was ignored and gained a tainted reputation. It became known as a dangerous area and derelicts had made it their home. For a period of time, the River Walk was declared off-limits to military personnel. Vandalism was prevalent and, once again, the river was regarded as a bad element of downtown.

During the late 1950's and early 1960's, Harold Robbins, then with the Chamber of Commerce, Robert Frazier, then Director of Parks and Recreation, and business leaders David

FOR DECADES, THE RIVER WALK ENJOYED LITTLE POPULARITY AND, AT TIMES, WAS EVEN OFF LIMITS TO THE MILITARY. HERE, TWO SAILORS PADDLE A CANOE BY AN EMPTY, GRAFFITI-SCARRED ARNESON RIVER THEATER. *Photo from the DRT Library at the Alamo*

WHILE THIS SOLDIER AND HIS DATE SEEM HAPPY ENOUGH PADDLING THEIR BOAT ALONG THE RIVER, THERE WERE PERIODS WHEN THE RIVER WALK WAS DECLARED OFF LIMITS TO MILITARY PERSONNEL BECAUSE IT WAS CONSIDERED TOO REMOTE AND DANGEROUS.
San Antonio Conservation Society Photo

THE TALL GIRLS SHOP WAS IN THE RIVERSIDE HOTEL BUILDING ON THE RIVER AT PRESA AND COLLEGE STREETS. A NIGHTCLUB LATER TOOK THE SPACE THAT IS NOW THE BAYOUS RESTAURANT ON STREET AND RIVER LEVELS, AND THE HOTEL IS NOW APARTMENTS.
Cy Wagner Photo

Straus and Arthur P. Veltman Jr. were instrumental in renewing interest in the River Walk among downtown businessmen.

The San Antonio Chamber of Commerce was able to raise $15,000 which was matched by the city for a feasibility study to determine the appropriate use of the River Bend area. The Marco Engineering Co. of California that had worked on Disneyland was hired as the study consultant and the firm's report strongly suggested that the River Bend area did, indeed, have great potential as a tourist attraction.

Through the efforts of Straus, the River Walk District and the River Walk Advisory Commission were created in 1962.

With backing from the Chamber of Commerce, the city commission convinced the San Antonio Chapter of American Institute of Architects to prepare a new master plan for the River Bend area.

Eventually, each property owner received recommendations on how to develop their holdings. A bond issue approved in January 1964 included $500,000 for river improvements.

Shortly thereafter, the Chamber of Commerce founded the Paseo del Rio Association, consisting of property owners and businessmen along the River Walk. Once again, a major effort to beautify the River Walk began.

A bridge was added in the River Bend between the Commerce and Crockett Street bridges. Another was added in front of the Hilton Palacio del Rio Hotel and another over a new river channel extended to the Convention Center that was built in 1967 as part of the preparations for HemisFair.

During San Antonio's second river renaissance, many dilapidated frame buildings along the River Walk were removed. Others were remodeled and their back doors facing the river became new front doors. Flowers and shrubs were planted. Once again, the River Walk was the centerpiece of downtown. The river was ready for millions of visitors from all over the world who were to come to San Antonio for HemisFair '68.

The Paseo del Rio is internationally known for its unique design and has been used as a model for development in other cities. Cities known to have studied the Paseo del Rio include Dayton, Ohio; Charlotte, North Carolina; Indianapolis, Indiana; Louisville, Kentucky; Reno, Nevada; Santa Cruz and Sacramento, California; Minneapolis, Phoenix, Houston and Ontario, Canada.

Although Hugman had no official connection with the River Walk after he was fired as project architect, he remained dedicated to its beautification throughout his lifetime. Hugman continued his practice as a architect in San Antonio. In 1957, he was hired at Randolph Air Force Base and worked there until 1972 on numerous projects, including designing flight simulator facilities.

EVEN AFTER ITS CONSTRUCTION, THE RIVER WALK WAS NOT WIDELY USED, AS SEEN IN THIS VIEW FROM ST. MARY'S STREET TOWARD NAVARRO STREET TAKEN AROUND 1950. LA MANSION DEL RIO HOTEL WAS LATER BUILT ON THE LEFT BANK BY THE FOOTBRIDGE.
San Antonio Light Photo

Still, he never forgot the river. Whenever construction or architectural changes were suggested for the River Walk, Hugman responded.

In February, 1972, he called for a forum when he heard of plans to change the Paseo del Rio into a loop by relocating a floodgate to a point further south on the river.

His major concern with relocating the floodgate was that the natural flow of the river would be curtailed, creating an irregular circular lake. He pointed out that the river bend was designed to allow water to flow slowly, and if this flow was deterred, seepage into nearby buildings might occur. This indeed happened when the floodgate was later removed, but the problem was also solved.

The point is that Hugman deeply cared about the River Walk even after all his official ties with it were severed. After all, it was the pinnacle of his professional achievements, had greatly affected his personal design philosophies, not to mention his entire life.

In March 9, 1976, he wrote an article published in the San Antonio Light expressing fear that the River Walk may be losing its aesthetic appeal. His concern at that time was the threat of future high-rise buildings casting shadows on the River Walk's lush greenery.

Hugman warned that the "Paseo del Rio will lose its sparkle." He added: "No, City Council members, do not give up a central city park for any construction purposes. If anything, gain more and zone the San Antonio River to protect and enhance its beauty for our citizens and tourists."

Earlier, he expressed his continuing concern that a balance be maintained between nature and commercial uses of the River Walk. He was quoted in the San Antonio Light on November 5, 1972: "What we have to decide, is whether Paseo del Rio is to be developed as the Venice of America or the Convention Center on a creek."

Hugman's dedication and concern for the quality of development along the River Walk remained a lifelong issue, as illustrated in his own words quoted in the San Antonio Light on May 19, 1974:

"I know that river. It's my baby. They used to call me Old Man River."

CHAPTER EIGHT

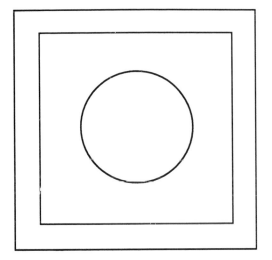

The Ceremony Of the Bells

On November 1, 1978, a ceremony was held in the Arneson River Theater honoring Robert Hugman for his contributions to San Antonio's River Walk.

The planners and participants in this ceremony must have given considerable thought as to how to appropriately honor a man who had given so much of himself to a concept he envisioned as a young man and which had so dominated most of his professional and private life.

Most words of praise chosen for carefully written speeches must have seemed rather superficial to those honoring Hugman on that day; his contributions had been of inestimable value to the River Walk development and had touched so many lives.

That Hugman's original River Walk concept had such tremendous impact on so many people since he first outlined the plan at that first meeting nearly 50 years earlier must have been a bit overwhelming for those trying to plan some appropriate tribute.

Two individuals most instrumental in organizing the ceremony were Mr. and Mrs. Frank W. Phelps, owners of two River Walk restaurants. Frank Phelps had learned of Hugman's original ideas and of his devotion to the River Walk through business associates and members of various organizations who shared an interest in saluting the man who designed the River Walk.

When Phelps learned Hugman's original scheme for the Arneson River Theater included bells in the arches of the stage backdrop, Phelps invited Hugman to dinner at one of his restaurants. During dinner discussions, Hugman affirmed his desire to have bells complete the Arneson River Theater.

"He was attentive, but somewhat skeptical of my intentions to finish the Arneson River Theater as he had planned it," said Phelps.

Later, when Phelps had Col. Carl J. Crane, the only licensed bell-maker in Texas, contact Hugman about the design of the bells, the architect suddenly became very enthusiastic.[50]

On June 23, 1978, Phelps called Crane, who used the trade name and title of Carlos Jose Garza, Bellmaker of Bexar, to discuss the design and casting of the bells for the Arneson. The next day, they inspected the arches designed into the rear stage wall of the open-air theater.

A photographed layout showing how the bells would look was presented to Phelps and to Tom Keeter, city parks supervisor.

Eventually, five bells were cast by Alamo Iron Works. The largest bell weighs 125 pounds and bears the following inscription:

"In honor of Robert H.H. Hugman, concept architect, San Antonio River."[51]

But permission to hang the bells and hold the ceremony took over two months. In the meantime, the bells were mounted from the ceiling of the Bombach House, also known

INSCRIPTION ON THE LARGEST ARNESON RIVER THEATER BELL SAYS: 'IN HONOR OF ROBERT H.H. HUGMAN, CONCEPT ARCHITECT SAN ANTONIO RIVER WALK.' THE DESIGNER WAS COL. CARL CRANE, KNOWN AS CARLOS JOSE GARZA, BELLMAKER OF BEXAR.
Photo by Col. Carl J. Crane

ROBERT HUGMAN PERSONALLY TESTS THE TIMBRE OF THE ARNESON RIVER THEATER BELLS AT THE ALAMO IRON WORKS FOUNDRY.
Photo by Col. Carl J. Crane

as Little Rhein steakhouse, where they immediately became a conversation piece.

According to the maitre d', customers were reluctant to take their seats until they were assured the bells would not fall. Some customers jokingly made comments such as "What are you doing, converting this place into a cathedral? Where are the bats?"[52]

Finally, Phelps, the Conservation Society, the Paseo del Rio Association, the local chapter of the American Institute of Architects, the San Antonio Chamber of Commerce, and the San Antonio Convention and Visitors' Bureau held the ceremony honoring Hugman.

After words of praise from several prominent citizens, including Mayor Lila Cockrell, Hugman presented a speech entitled, "How Paseo del Rio."

Hugman began his remarks with a brief summary of events following the 1921 flood. In a section entitled "Mama says, No!" Hugman credited the women of the city with successfully thwarting plans to turn the River Bend into a drainage ditch.

Hugman noted the difficulty in obtaining funds for the river project during the Depression and how hotel entrepreneur Jack White promoted the plan and obtained the necessary funding through the WPA.

He then told an amusing story about Dwight D. Book, owner of the Book Building at Houston Street and the river, who strongly objected to any construction on his property. Book's attitude, as recalled by Hugman, was:

"The river project will never amount to a hill of beans, and if you ever see more than two people walking on the River Walk at any one time, I'll eat your hat."

Hugman went to see Book to try to convince him that the planned river improvements would enhance his property.

"We started by having a small glass of wine in his office, then we went to a couple of bars around the corner. The old rascal knew exactly what I wanted of him, and he played me like a fish on a line. About 5:30 p.m., after wine, beer, ale, and eggs, I said, 'Colonel, I must go but before I do, I want you to tell me you will call off the dogs and stop objecting to my river plans.' In a fine and mellow mood by this time, he straightened up at the bar and said, 'I now appoint you official architect for the Book Building, and if you look out for my interest, I will do as you wish.' I walked, unsure of my steps but pleased, back to my office. The next day I reported to Jack White."

Hugman then talked about the breakthrough of the bond-issue passage and detailed how parts of the construction were actually done.

He proudly noted that the River Walk was regarded as one of the most outstanding WPA projects in the nation, adding praise for Robert Turk's excellent work as project superintendent.

"Mr. Turk and I soon learned that while we were discussing river work, all the workmen within earshot would stop and listen intently to our conversation. We then purposely

FRANK W. PHELPS ACCEPTS THE ARNESON RIVER THEATER BELLS FROM ALAMO IRON WORKS.   *Photo from Frank W. Phelps*

ROBERT HUGMAN AND MAYOR LILA COCKRELL, CENTER, PULL ROPES TO RING THE LARGEST OF THE ARNESON RIVER THEATER BELLS INSTALLED AS A TRIBUTE TO HUGMAN IN CEREMONIES IN 1978 -- AN EVENT THAT DREW EXTENSIVE NEWS MEDIA COVERAGE.
The Institute of Texan Cultures

talked loud enough for them to hear and understand. They would then return to their work with added vigor and purpose. Mr Turk and I believed the workmen's understanding and interest contributed greatly to the work accomplished."

Hugman also praised Ed Arneson for whom the river theater was named, calling him "a respected engineer and a prince of a man."

Arneson was the chief engineer in charge of the WPA district office and was an enthusiastic supporter of the River Walk project, although he died before the work got under way.

When speaking of the water control structures built as part of the project, Hugman explained that they were not only designed for flood control, but also to provide an even and gentle flow of water through the Paseo del Rio.

The downstream control structure, located near the Plaza Hotel — now the Granada Apartments — was designed to raise the water level to approximately six feet and, by maintaining a constant water level, walkways could then be constructed.

Hugman had consistently recommended a water depth of 3.5 feet, saying that would prevent drownings and still allow small passenger boats to be used.

But silt eventually accumulated in the river bottom, so the water depth was increased. Still, Hugman made it clear he preferred maintaining a slow tempo and a romantic atmosphere and that pole-powered boats would be better than motorized ones.

"Who needs noise in the Paseo del Rio world?" he asked.

Gondolas were part of Hugman's original vision of the Shops of Aragon and Romula and related one of the early reactions to his idea:

"I called on a public official in 1929 who was a very smart businessman, but had little formal education. I told him of my dreams for developing the river . . . and I mentioned gondolas quietly gliding on the water as a part of an imaginary setting. He thought the entire idea was fine, but then he said, 'Oh, we won't need to buy many gondolas, we can get a pair and raise our own.'"

Hugman lauded David Straus' leadership in focusing new attention on the river in the 1960's. He also mentioned the outstanding work of parks director Robert Frazier for giving the River Walk a manicured look.

On the future of the River Walk, Hugman said the ideal "will be to look backward for a certain historic character that is peculiarly San Antonio's own; thus to build an additional aesthetic character and color based upon Spanish, Mexican, and Southwest traditions. Our little river needs to be considered as a stage setting in which people are transported to the unusual. Unusual shops, unusual landscaping, color and modes of transportation. The greatest need for the future is to not go modern in architectural styles, but to guard jealously the river tempo, slow and lazy, in complete contrast with the hustle and bustle of street-level modern city life."

After these final thoughts, Hugman rang the largest of the bells along with Mayor Lila Cockrell. His speech had basically supported the original vision created in 1929 of the Shops of Aragon and Romula.

The speech suggested Hugman felt his task was finally complete.

On November 3, 1978, Hugman was honored at the 39th annual meeting of the Texas Society of Architects and was presented a certificate of honor for his design and planning of the River Walk.

Although not formally honored until November 1978, Hugman had received increased recognition for his contributions to the River Walk in the early 1970's.

Several articles appeared in local newspapers suggesting Hugman be given more credit. Typical was an article by Norma Reed in The San Antonio Light October 16, 1978:

"Today, the river is bringing San Antonio numerous large national conventions and publicity from all media. Credit for the river beautification is usually handed to Maverick, White or both. But, in the publicity of the river, Hugman is seldom mentioned. This seems a shame, since the River Bend, as it exists now, was conceived by Hugman 41 years ago, even down to its immense possibilities as a national tourist attraction."

Reed wrote that she had contacted Hugman and he said he was happy about how the Paseo del Rio had turned out, but noted he "shrugs off the fact that he is seldom mentioned in connection with it. But, he wouldn't be human if he weren't a little disappointed at a city adopting an idea so completely and, just as completely, forgetting the man who gave it to them."

At the same time, Hugman had become increasingly concerned with documenting the history of the River Walk.

On April 11, 1966, Hugman wrote to Conservation Society President Mrs. Don Tobin, urging the society to preserve all records of the River Walk project.

He noted that an article in the March 1966 Reader's Digest, entitled "They Bring Back Yesterdays," was not completely accurate concerning how the downtown river was saved.

He then explained: "To conserve means to preserve, and to preserve historical facts should rank along with places and things; therefore, I call your organization's attention to the need for the compiling of factual data regarding the San Antonio River development."[53]

Another of Hugman's concerns was giving proper recognition to those in the late 1920's and early 1930's who helped promote his River Walk ideas.

He lauded Mrs. Lane Taylor for strongly opposing proposals to cover over the River Bend.

He also felt that others, such as river committee members Claud V. Birkhead and Isaac Bledsoe, should be recognized for their unpaid service and contributions. Some years after his 1966 letter noting that records had not been kept document-

HUGMAN SMILES DURING 1978 CEREMONIES SALUTING HIS WORK AS THE RIVER WALK'S PLANNER AND DESIGNER. MAYOR LILA COCKRELL, RIGHT, AND CONSERVATION SOCIETY PRESIDENT MARY ANN CASTLEBERRY, LEAD THE TRIBUTE AT THE ARNESON RIVER THEATER WHERE A SET OF BELLS WAS DEDICATED IN HUGMAN'S HONOR. *San Antonio Conservation Society Photo*

ing the true history of the River Walk development, Hugman compiled a summary of the project and sent it to the San Antonio Conservation Society for its archives.

The River Walk has, indeed, emerged as a unique and unusual development in the center of a downtown metropolitan area. Its architectural and landscape design express an aesthetic unity that contrasts with the hurried tempo and urban confusion of downtown streets.

The informal landscape design complements the pace of the slow-moving water. The balance that has evolved among parkland, entertainment, dwellings and business enterprises manifests the diversity that was the very core of Hugman's plan.

In the fall of 1970 and summer of 1971, a team of researchers from Texas A&M University interviewed 720 people on the River Walk at nine survey points.

The survey showed a majority see the River Walk as beautiful, interesting and charming. They did not view the commercial and non-commercial elements of the River Walk as separate. Thus, the public affirms the premise Hugman first offered in the late 1920's — that public and private development can and must achieve a balance.

The aesthetic appeal of the river was his major theme, but he also emphasized its commercial potential.

"To me, the river is one of nature's greatest gifts to San Antonio and should be appreciated and developed as such. Our city is the mecca for thousands of tourists each year, not only because of its wonderful climate, but because of its atmosphere."

The ceremony of the bells at the Arneson River Theater was a formal way of honoring Hugman for his achievements. No doubt, Hugman was very appreciative, particularly of the five bells that had been mounted in the arches he prepared for them almost four decades earlier.

The news coverage, expressions of appreciation from speakers and the audience reaction at the Ceremony of the Bells undoubtedly reinforced Hugman's sense of accomplishment. Earlier that same week, he had been bestowed the title of "Father of the River Walk."

Interestingly, Hugman was a very private person who shared his thoughts with only a few. Although he enjoyed public recognition, his greatest sense of achievement seemed to come from personally watching the River Walk evolve. As the unique character of the river unfolded and was recognized as an outstanding piece of urban design, he saw his dream come true.

Renewed interest in the River Walk in the late 1960's was an exciting experience for him. A new generation had emerged full of energy and enthusiasm about carrying out and improving on what had become Hugman's quest in life.

The vicarious satisfaction of watching another unusual shop, restaurant, apartment building or garden evolve from idea to reality on the river was, at least, partial repayment to a man earlier left feeling only humiliation and despair.

Victory was his in the end. He not only had prevailed, but was duly honored, not only locally, but with prestigious national design tributes and even international acclaim.

When Hugman strolled the River Walk near the end of his life, he had to have seen what pleasure his River Walk was giving to so many people.

Surely, he witnessed the excited face of a young child, the couple enjoying the park-like serenity, the out-of-state visitor marvelling at the semi-tropical plants, the apartment-dweller savoring the view from a riverside balcony, an individual lost for a few minutes in a relaxing dream world while seated on a bench by the sparkling water, teen-agers holding hands in the romantic setting he had created, heard the applause of an audience delighted by a performance under the stars at the Arneson River Theater.

All this and more, were Hugman's reward.

Comments like these from the Texas A&M survey in 1970 and 1971 must have pleased the man who "created" and "invented' the River Walk:

"Atmosphere of old Mexico, although different."

"Clean, green atmosphere; helps relax — like a vacation spot in the middle of town."

"Attractive, quiet, unique."

"Calmness, quietness, scenery."

"Outdoor restaurants and landscape."

"Lots of good views, pleasant to walk along, peaceful, no cares, fact that there is a river."

"Beautiful, Spanish culture, not too commercial."

"Its aesthetic quality, lush landscaping, friendly relaxed people and interesting shops."

"Designed in a sense that keeps human proportions, not regimented; not a national park, but commercial and natural — takes into account all human activities: dining, nightlife, relaxing, fact is downtown but completely divorced from city; like in the country."

"Romantic atmosphere."

"The variety of ways to relax and the different things to do on the River Walk; it gives relief to the flat topography of the area."

"The exotic, somewhat European, flavor and the exciting atmosphere."

"Very attractive to tourists, and adds a romantic character to the city."

But the quotation that must have pleased him most came from an astute observer, who said simply:

"It is San Antonio."[54]

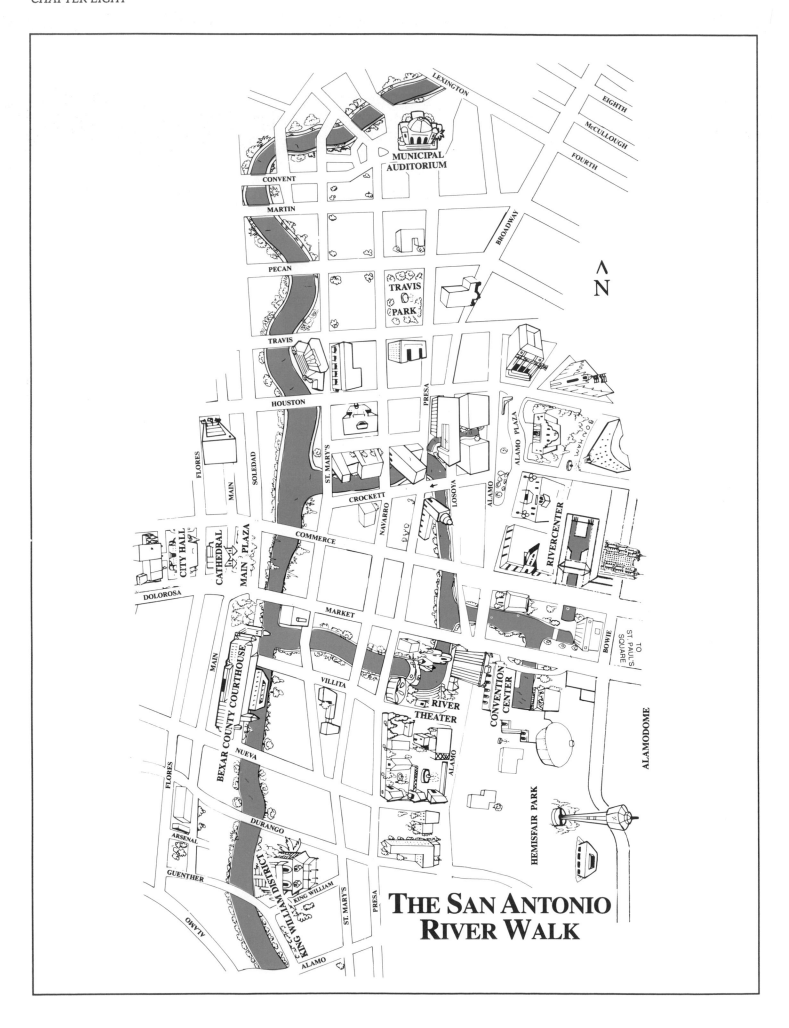

**THE SAN ANTONIO
RIVER WALK**

CHAPTER NINE

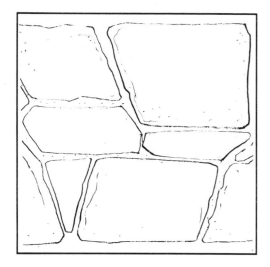

Hugman Looks Back At His Masterpiece

The following is the text of Hugman's speech, "How Paseo del Rio" given at the Ceremony of the Bells at the Arneson River Theater, November 1, 1978:

THE FLOOD

The year was 1929 when there was much to-do about the river. Because of the 1921 flood, which put nine feet of water on Houston Street downtown, the city had to do something about flooding. Engineers were employed and the plan was to build the Olmos Dam with its retention basin and next to take the excessive meanderings out of the San Antonio River between Olmos Dam and the Central City, then to build the channel cut-off from north of Commerce Street to Villita Street so flood waters would not be forced through the Horseshoe Bend or Big Bend you visualize today as Paseo del Rio.

MAMA SAYS, 'NO'

The Olmos Dam was built; two or three river meanderings were removed above the central city, one being the area on which the Municipal Auditorium was built. When it came to eliminating the Big Bend in the heart of the city, the prominent club (wives of leading businessmen) of our city said, "No!" The flood control engineers proposed the abandonment of the Big Bend section of the river and the businessmen approved the idea because it would be paved over, become another street with underground local drainage, thus making their property more valuable because of the second frontage.

The ladies, with their keen aesthetic taste, wanted to preserve the "little river." At this point in time, after the University of Texas, marriage and three and one-half years in New Orleans, I returned to San Antonio, my home town, and had gone into business as an architect. While in New Orleans, I was impressed by the "Old World charm, beauty, local color and character" of it all. It was at this time that the leaders of New Orleans were so wisely beginning to preserve their Vieux Carre District.

DINNER WILL BE LATE

Because of the excitement about the flood control program and the elimination of the Big Bend in the river, I began to think about the problem. I had an idea!

I went to see Mrs. Lane Taylor, a lovely and gracious lady who was the president of the San Antonio Conservation Society at the time. It was four o'clock in the afternoon and Mrs. Taylor and I talked until about six when Mr. Taylor arrived. He was greeted with, "Lane, your dinner will be a little late this evening. We have plans for the river."

I then prepared a hand-lettered brochure of my dream on parchment paper and placed it in a handmade leather cover. This brochure I personally presented to about 100 prominent people in San Antonio who endorsed it as the future plan for the Big Bend.

Here are a few of the names in the '29 era: Mayor C. M. Chambers and his Commissioners, S. W. Freese, Albert Steves, R. W. Morrison, J. K. Beretta, F. L. Hillyer, Walter P. Napier, Reagan Houston, Thomas J. Hart, W. W. McAllister, Amanda C. Taylor, Ernest R. Brown, Mrs. Frank N. Sorell, C. A. Wheatley, C. M. Tobin, O. P. Schnabel, Elizabeth O. Graham.

Names appearing in the '39 era: Mayor C. K. Quin and his Commissioners Isaac Bledsoe, Claude V. Birkhead to mention only a few names at random, plus Gutzon Borglum, (the sculptor who designed Mount Rushmore) who lived and worked in San Antonio for a time.

City officials and engineers all approved my water-level shop development plan which I called Shops of Aragon and Romula. Signatures I got, but there was no monetary way to realize such a river development. However, the Big Bend was not filled in and made into a street; the channel cut-off was built and the horseshoe bend in the river did remain as it was.

ROBERT HUGMAN WHEN HE WAS HONORED.
Photo from Elene Hugman

THE DEPRESSION ERA

The severe national depression of 1929 and early 30's did not hit San Antonio hard until about 1934. In '36, we had many "make work" projects in Bexar County. Local attorneys, architects, engineers and other professional people, including myself, worked on various "make work" projects. One day Mr. Jack White, then Manager of the Plaza Hotel, went to City Hall to see if the city would, "clean up the dirty little river" next to the hotel property. At that meeting, an old San Antonian (a Canary Islander) by the name of John Richter told Mr. White about my plans for the river. Mr. White got in touch with me and as I was working for the WPA, under Mr. Ed Arneson the District No. 10 Director, we began to think of another "make work" project — the Central City river.

Sketches by me, and estimates of cost by others in the WPA office, were made. We determined that the river project from Fourth Street on the north and south to the lower end of the Big Bend would cost about $380,000, but the city would need to be the sponsor and put up $75,000.

The city could not supply the money at the time, so Mr. White and Committees of the Chamber of Commerce helped to work out other schemes for raising the $75,000. It was decided to set up a Bonded District consisting of a block on each side of the river course to be improved. The law stated "Property owners must also live within the district to be eligible to vote." It was found there were only five people really opposed to the development.

Others who owned property within the district, but did not live there, also opposed the project. Among these, was a colorful character by the name of D.D. Book who owned the red brick building on the southwest corner of Houston Street and the river.

MR. BOOK

When the gentlemen from the Chamber of Commerce called on Mr. Book, he told them, "If anyone puts an obstruction to flooding, even one cubic foot, in the sacred San Antonio River Channel, I'll sue."

When Mr. White learned of this, and other negative reactions, he began looking for someone who knew "old man Book." Jack called me and said, "I hear you know Mr. Book. Will you try to get him to withdraw his objections?" Mr. Book and I enjoyed an unusual friendship based upon our mutual interest in inventing, and his knowledge of my proposals for the river in 1929. He had said to me, "Colonel, the river project will never amount to a 'hill of beans' and if you ever see more than two people walking on the River Walk at any one time, I'll eat your hat."

Well, when Jack White called me, I went to see my friend during his office hours which were, as he said, between 3:00 and 3:15 p.m. almost daily because, really, he was old, wealthy and retired. From time to time, Mr. Book would come by to see me, take me out for oysters, beer or to La Louisiane. As I said, we were simpatico.

We started by having a small glass of wine in his office, then to a couple of bars 'round the corner. The old rascal knew exactly what I wanted of him, and he played me like a fish on a line. About 5:30 p.m., after wine, beer, ale and eggs, I said, "Colonel, I must go, but before I do, I want you to tell me you will call off the dogs and stop objecting to my river plans." In a fine and mellow mood, by this time, he straightened up at the bar and said, "I now appoint you official architect for the Book Building, and if you look out for my interest, I will do as you wish."

I walked, unsure of my steps but pleased, back to my office. The next day I reported to Jack White.

THE BOND ISSUE

Since one had to live in the district in order to vote on the Bond Issue and two of the five land owners were opposed to it, the scheme was devised to have people living in the Plaza Hotel vote. If they owned personal property consisting of as much as a watch, they were technically qualified to vote. The outcome of the voting in District 15 was in favor of the bond 74 to 2.

Now with success in view, I was employed by the city as architect and Mr. Ed Arneson as the engineer for the project. A River Advisory Committee was formed consisting of Jack White, Isaac Bledsoe, Judge Claude V. Birkhead, Dr. F. G. Oppenheimer, D. A. Powell, Wilbur Matthews, W. W. McAllister and Father Arnold.

My task was to prepare all architectural and landscaping plans. Mr. Ed Arneson was to prepare the structural and engineering drawings. Unfortunately, Ed was unable to proceed because of illness and died shortly thereafter.

FOR YEARS, A DEPRESSING SLUM-LIKE ADDITION OF CORRUGATED METAL FACED THE RIVER WALK JUST NORTH OF COMMERCE STREET.
San Antonio Magazine Photo

IMPROVEMENTS TURNED THE FORMER BACK DOOR INTO A NUMBER OF RIVER VIEW ROOMS AND BALCONIES FOR ADJOINING BUSINESSES AND AN ICE CREAM SHOPPE OPERATED AT RIVER LEVEL. HERE, A CUSTOMER RIDING A PADDLE BOAT HAS STOPPED FOR A SCOOP OR TWO.
Photo from Frank W. Phelps

FURTHER IMPROVEMENTS TO THE RIVER SIDE OF THE ROW OF HISTORIC BUILDINGS ALONG COMMERCE STREET PRODUCED THIS NEW
ARCHED FACADE OVERLOOKING A RIVER WALK PATIO.
San Antonio Magazine Photo

THE ARCHED RIVER PATIO NOW HAS TWO LEVELS AND SERVES RIO RIO CANTINA UPSTAIRS AND BOUDRO'S DOWNSTAIRS, WHICH
FEATURES ORIGINAL-DESIGN 'POTATO CHIP' UMBRELLAS ALONG THE EDGE OF THE RIVER.
David Anthony Richelieu Photo

Mr. W.H. Lilly assumed Mr. Arneson's engineering respon-
sibilities and prepared the structural drawings for this project.
After all architectural design, landscaping and structural working drawings were completed, they were approved by the City
Engineer, Tom Coghill, and by Jack White, chairman of the
committee.

WORK BEGAN

Mr. H.P. Drought, Sr. was state administrator when the WPA
work was started by the district office. It should be noted that
this project was known as one of the most outstanding WPA
Projects in the nation as to the amount of work accomplished
per dollar expended. This was possible because many men
could work in many areas at the same time and under the ex-
pert guidance of an excellent superintendent, Mr. Robert H.
Turk.

Mr. Turk and I soon learned that while we discussed "river
work" all the workmen within earshot would stop and listen
intently to our conversation.

We then purposely talked loud enough for them to hear
and understand. They would then return to their work with
added vigor and purpose. Mr. Turk and I believe the
workmen's understanding and interest contributed greatly to
the work accomplished.

THE CONSTRUCTION ERA

After all the flood engineering, financial, political, organi-
zational and personal involvements, the central city river beautification WPA Project work gets under way. We were no more
than started when an injunction suit was slapped on us, but
this was of short duration and, after a little show of force, work
continued.

At the end of this story and review of events, a list of local
newspaper headlines is given so you may get a running out-
line of actual events; however, I will proceed to expand a few
of those having a bearing on the late '30 and '40 construction
era.

THE RIVER THEATER

Before the WPA river project started in 1939, restoration of
La Villita got under way and was developed as another "make
work project" through the Youth Corps and under the guidance of Mayor Maury Maverick. As part of the La Villita land-
assembling venture, the ground now the seating area of the
Arneson River Theater was acquired in conjunction with the
old Cos House.

The Cos House was restored under the Youth Corps La
Villita Project, but the complete river theater was my design
and built by the WPA. There were to have been five bells in
the arches behind the stage, but this feature was never realized. Perhaps by the next time you visit Paseo del Rio, the
bells will ring for you; yes, and for me, too.

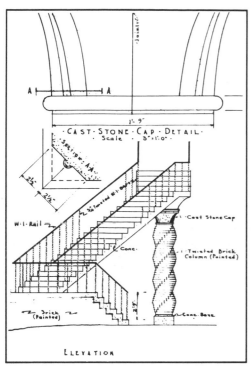

HUGMAN'S DRAWING DETAIL OF HIS TWISTED STAIR-SUPPORT COLUMN EXECUTED IN BRICK.

HUGMAN'S STAIR COLUMN AS SEEN TODAY BY TOURISTS BY THE CROCKETT STREET BRIDGE.
David Anthony Richelieu Photo

I am getting away from my story. In the La Villita area, there were several machine shops and, you guessed it, the river bank was the dumping ground for old auto and machine parts. Mr. Turk and his men removed many tons of machine parts, grease and car frames from the river bank where you may now sit to enjoy theater performances.

As you may know, Mr. Ed Arneson was a local engineer who directed the District Office of the WPA in the '30's. The Regional WPA was directed by Mr. H. P. Drought, Sr., a local attorney. What you may not know is that Ed was greatly beloved, as he was not only a widely respected engineer, but a prince of a man. When the work was well along and the River Theater began to take shape, Mr. Drought proposed the theater be named after Mr. Ed Arneson, and so it is known today.

CONTROL STRUCTURES

The 10-block waterway of Paseo del Rio naturally flowed gently form north to south. The structure at the south end raised the old water level about six feet so there would only be less than a foot fall from the north to the south end. The water control structure with five original arched openings at the upstream end of the Big Bend is designed with steel down-sliding gates to prevent flood waters from entering the Paseo del Rio waterway. The water level control structure at the downstream end of the Big Bend was designed to raise the old water level about six feet. Both of these structures cause the water to flow gently through Paseo Del Rio and thus establish level walkways.

WATER DEPTH

In the Big Bend there were both deep and shallow places, so a depth of 3.5 feet was established by excavating and filling in where needed. At this depth, drowning should not take place, and during WW II, there was a concession to rent canoes on the river. The river depth was tested many times. When a large crowd gathered on a bridge, you could bet a canoe had capsized. The soldiers delighted in taking their girlfriends for a ride and, if they were not careful, over they went. The soldiers thought it was great, but the girl would come out sputtering, holding her purse and hat high while the spectators laughed.

The water depth was also established so passenger carrying boats could be poled along as in Xochimilco, Mexico, for color and a slow tempo. There is no place to go and nobody is in a hurry to get there. This was done in the early 1940's. Silt was allowed to accumulate in the river bottom and the boats could not be poled along. I believe it would be much more romantic and appropriate to so propel boats along today — who needs noise in the Paseo del Rio world?

STAIRWAYS

As you walk or ride along Paseo del Rio, you may observe many designs in stairways. Each of these had to be especially

THIS WAS THE UNATTRACTIVE BACK DOOR THAT PRESA STREET BUILDINGS PRESENTED TO THE RIVER FOR YEARS UNTIL HEMISFAIR '68.
Photo from Arthur P. Veltman Jr.

THE SLUM-LIKE AREA WAS TRANSFORMED BY CONSTRUCTION OF RIVER SQUARE, HOME OF THE KANGAROO COURT AND OTHER BUSINESSES THAT HAVE SINCE MADE THIS THE BUSIEST STRETCH OF THE ENTIRE RIVER WALK.
Photo from Arthur P. Veltman Jr.

A RIVER WALK RENAISSANCE BEGAN IN EARNEST WITH RIVER SQUARE CONSTRUCTION AROUND THE TIME OF HEMISFAIR THAT ALSO INCLUDED THIS NEW ARCHED FOOTBRIDGE OVER THE RIVER.
Photo from Frank W. Phelps

A JUMBLE OF COURTYARDS FILLED WITH COLORFUL UMBRELLAS, NUMEROUS STAIRS, PASSAGEWAYS, INTERESTING SHOPS, BUILDINGS WITH SOARING ARCHES AND OTHER FEATURES HAVE HELPED MAKE THE RIVER SQUARE BLOCK THE VERY CROSSROADS OF THE RIVER WALK.
David Anthony Richelieu Photo

designed for a water-soaked earth and vibrating bridges on existing street-level structures. The foundations under the stairways are very heavy and stairways placed on top are similar to a tea kettle with a long spout. The variously designed stairways are self supporting (cantilevered) and are not attached to street level structures.

BRIDGES

You will notice two lovely tile plaques located on the walls. One at the Navarro Street Bridge reads:

"Navarro St. Bridge, WPA - 1942, Old Mill Crossing Plaque, Last known place where horses drank and forded the river. Dedicated to the memory of our fathers — Erected by the Daughters of Texas Trail Drivers."

The other plaque is located at the control structure, upstream end of the Big Bend near the still-standing twin cypress trees and reads:

"An old legend describes this twin cypress as a lookout of a Mexican sniper who picked off the Texans as they came to the river for water."

These tile plaques were made by another WPA Project and supervised by a Mrs. Harris. She and her workers used a small rock house on North St. Mary's Street where the Southwestern Bell Telephone Company building now stands at McCullough Avenue. Mrs. Harris later became custodian of San Jose Mission.

FRESH WATER LOBSTERS

The old river waterway through the Big Bend area was everybody's backyard. Some cypress, cottonwood, elm and anaqua (sugarberry) trees grew naturally. There was grass in spots and the normal water channel was lined with dilapidated rock walls.

When these old walls were removed, a family or nest of fresh water lobsters was found by the workmen. (If you have visited the Little Rhine Steak House, that is the area where they were found.) Mr. Jack White had put the word out that all relics found were to be turned over to him. When the lobsters were found the "boys" did not consider them relics, so the "boys" could not find them when a request was made for them.

GONDOLAS

One experience I must mention, goes as follows: I called on a public official in 1929 who was a very smart businessman, but (had) little formal education. I told him of my dreams for developing the river called The Shops of Aragon and Romula (for lack of a better name, and it did sound romantic) and I mentioned gondolas quietly gliding on the water as part of an imaginary setting. He thought the entire idea was fine, but then he said "Oh, we won't need to buy many gondolas, we can buy a pair and raise our own."

After Casa Rio Restaurant opened a half-block downstream, this barbecue eatery opened on the river below Losoya Street. Despite wagon-wheel railings and other Western touches, it didn't last long. *Casa Rio Restaurant Photo*

In its second life, the site was operated as Venice Restaurant. Today, it remains an Italian restaurant, Michelino's, one of three in the same triangular shaped building at Losoya Street and the river. *Photo from Cy Wagner*

FIRST RIVER OFFICE

As soon as the river walkway was finished, I opened my office at water level. The location was in the half circular space in the basement of the Old Riverside Building at the northwest corner of the Commerce Street Bridge. When I did this, people said, in essence; "I knew you were a dreamer, but now I know you are also a fool. You'll be drowned like a rat in your own hole." But, as you can plainly see, I was not.

PRESENT

From about the year 1950 until 1968, the original river development fell into disuse and abuse because there were insufficient shops, lighting, policing and care to make it really used by the public. When HemisFair was planned, Paseo del Rio really came into its own and I felt greatly gratified to see the many shops open on the river. One of my original sketches depicted the block from Crockett Street to Commerce Street developed as Foods of All Nations and that is almost what it turned out to be.

In the HemisFair planning era, many businessmen led by Mr. David Straus and a group of local architects contributed greatly to make Paseo del Rio what it is today. The well-kept, clean and manicured look of the river and its banks is due to an outstanding job by Bob Frazier, director of parks. Now that HemisFair is over, the focal point of all central city development is the river; thus you will see that after many trials and tribulations, the "little river" has come into its own and has become a benefactor to all of San Antonio.

MY WORK OVER

My professional work terminated with the completion of all control structures, stairways, bridges, walks and the Arneson River Theater, plus about half of the work between the north end of the Big Bend and the Fourth Street Bridge. I did not get to complete the supervision of my entire project for political reasons. You know, a poor boy does not fight City Hall.

THE FUTURE

In my opinion, the ideal future of Paseo del Rio will be to look backward for a certain historic character that is peculiarly San Antonio's own; thus to build-in additional aesthetic character and color based upon our Spanish, Mexican and Southwest traditions. Our "little river" needs be considered as a stage setting on which people are transported to the unusual. Unusual shops, unusual landscaping, color and modes of transportation.

The greatest need for the future is to not go modern in architectural styles, but to guard jealously the river tempo, slow and lazy, in complete contrast with the hustle and bustle of street-level modern city life.

IN THE EARLY 1940's, HUGMAN OPENED THE FIRST COMMERCIAL OFFICE ON THE RIVER WALK IN THE LOWER LEVEL OF THE CLIFFORD BUILDING AT COMMERCE STREET. HUGMAN'S ORIGINAL OFFICE SIGN SEEN ACROSS THE BALCONY FASCIA HAS RECENTLY BEEN RESTORED.

Photo from Anne Hugman Robinson

THE JOHN TWOHIG HOUSE WAS BUILT IN THE 1840'S ON THE RIVER WHERE IT CURVED EAST TOWARD THE RIVER BEND. THE BRIDGE AT RIGHT CONNECTED THE HOUSE TO TWOHIG'S BUSINESS ON COMMERCE STREET. THE HOUSE HAS BEEN RELOCATED TO THE WITTE MUSEUM GROUNDS AND RESTORED AND THIS SITE IS NOW THE BACK OF THE GARAGE OF THE FORMER PETROLEUM COMMERCE BUILDING.
The Institute of Texan Cultures

CHAPTER TEN

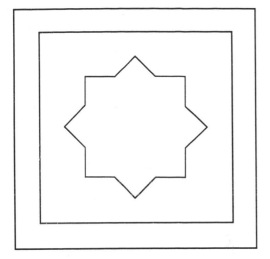

A Stroll on the River Walk in the 1990's

The River Walk concept that Hugman created has bolstered San Antonio's international acclaim as one of America's unique cities. However, Hugman emphasized that he alone should not receive credit for this accomplishment; many individuals and groups have contributed to the development of the River Walk. On many occasions, Hugman directed his comments to future generations who will determine the course the river will take in the next decades.

Today, there is every indication that development will continue along the banks of the San Antonio River and in surrounding neighborhoods and business districts. Hugman instinctively feared that uncontrolled future development might change the critical balance between commercial and non-commercial use of the River Walk.

Hugman's original vision of the river that he tirelessly mapped out before innumerable officials and civic groups, portrayed the river as having a unique character that must be maintained and safeguarded.

The rich historical legacy of the San Antonio River was a major part of what Hugman regarded as its unique character.

He strongly believed that periodic and systematic observation of the river would be the firmest foundation for planning its future. Thus, through observing the river and documenting its history, the river's real character would be preserved.

A look at the Paseo del Rio in the 1990's provides an opportunity to determine how well Hugman's concepts and ideas have endured.

We begin our observations with another river stroll, starting at the flood gates off West Commerce Street where the River Bend starts.

On the north bank is an inlaid tile mosaic depicting a Mexican sniper aiming his rifle at an unsuspecting Texan. It is said that the Mexican sniper who shot Ben Milam in the head during the Battle of San Antonio in 1835 had been perched in the fork of the branches of a large cypress in this area of the river. The site where Milam was shot is about a half-block north on the main channel and on the opposite side of the river.

Meanwhile, adjacent to the tile mural is an office building that once was the headquarters of City Public Service, the city-owned gas and electric utility. In recent years, it had been an office building known as the Petroleum Commerce Building. Perhaps typical of earlier times, the building's attached parking garage fronts on a stretch of the river. Both the building and garage are being remodeled into a small upscale hotel.

The building is on the original site where the John Twohig house was built in the 1840's. The house was dismantled in 1943 and moved to the grounds of the Witte Museum.

ORIGINAL ST. MARY'S ACADEMY INCLUDED MANSARD-STYLE BUILDINGS DESIGNED BY ARCHITECT, AND LATER MAYOR, FRANCOIS GIRAUD.
Photo from Patrick Kennedy

COLLEGE STREET FACADE OF COMPLEX AFTER IT BECAME ST. MARY'S COLLEGE. AFTER SERVING FOR DECADES AS THE ST. MARY'S LAW SCHOOL, THE HISTORIC COMPLEX WAS RENOVATED IN THE 1960'S INTO WHAT IS NOW THE LUXURIOUS LA MANSION DEL RIO HOTEL.
Photo from Patrick Kennedy

Midway between the flood gates and the St. Mary's Bridge, Twohig constructed a footbridge which he used as an access to his place of business on Commerce Street. Twohig was a banker and became well-known in early San Antonio for his generosity to the poor. Each Saturday evening he distributed bread to the needy, earning himself the nickname of the "Breadline Banker."

Strolling along the pebbled walkways, it is hard not to notice they are decorated with a variety of what look like inlaid designs.

The design shapes were created using wood-press forms that smoothed the surface of the wet concrete under the pattern. There are at least 10 different designs used along the walks, some alternating with plain panels, some in long runs of one pattern and some in special small sections.

The panels were poured in place and while they weren't intended to be "modular," they almost are. When repairs are done to the River Walk, panels are lifted out by crane, stacked up and then lifted back in. They are not steel reinforced, so some crack, but most do not and even broken ones usually can be easily repaired.

The sidewalk panels also reveal another of Hugman's design secrets for the River Walk. His entire plan was based on a diversity of shapes and forms but which all speak the same romantic Spanish architectural language. And so it is with his pebble-finished concrete walks along the river.

During their construction, he would have some of his female acquaintances test the walkways by wearing different styled shoes. Mrs. David Jones remembers that she and her mother took such "test walks" with Hugman.

"His dream was to make the River Walk attractive to all people, and he loved showing it off." Of Hugman's attention to the design of each sidewalk panel, Mrs. Jones said, "He wanted to make certain it was smooth enough for the women's high-heeled shoes." [55]

After passing under the St. Mary's Street Bridge, La Mansion del Rio Hotel comes into view. St. Mary's College once occupied these grounds. It was established in 1852 and opened on March 1, 1853, to 100 students. Some of those students came by boats that were tied to a landing located on the north bank near the base of an arched footbridge designed by Hugman.

The original facade featured a French-style mansard roof and gables. The original building was designed by architect Francois Giraud, who was also the architect for the Ursuline Academy, now the Southwest Craft Center, and for the Gothic addition to the front of San Fernando Cathedral.

Giraud also did the survey work mapping out the location of the original walls of the Alamo compound and eventually served as Mayor of San Antonio for two terms.

His same style was followed during several additions to St. Mary's over the years. In the early 1920's, St. Mary's College was moved and St. Mary's Academy was established at the location. From 1934 to 1963, the building housed the St. Mary's Law School.

At the time of HemisFair, the historic buildings were renovated into La Mansion del Rio Hotel. The complex received a six-story addition and the architectural style was changed to its present Spanish motif. Another addition was completed in December 1979.

As a graduate of the St. Mary's Law School formerly on the site, La Mansion's principal developer Patrick Kennedy had more than just a business interest in the historic structure.

When one of his daughters was born at the Nix Hospital across the street, Kennedy was gazing out of the hospital window of his wife's room, then turned and told her he wanted to purchase his former law school building and turn it into a first-class hotel.

It wasn't long before another dream came true on the River Walk.

Kennedy recently purchased a four-story turn-of-the-century furniture store directly across the river from La Mansion and plans to renovate it into a small luxury wing of the main hotel.

This new hotel wing sits above a half-block-long arcade built in 1988 using Hugman's original blueprints. Hugman's original stone arch wall was never built by the WPA, but, in 1987, funds from the city and the Conservation Society helped secure a federal Economic Development Administration grant for the construction, which cost close to $1 million.

The project was done, in part, to allow access through Hugman's arches to restaurants, shops and other retail activity under Crockett Street, which is parallel and directly next to the River Walk in that block.

The proposed River Walk connection through the arches also can extend to the basements of buildings on the south side of Crockett Street, including the restored Aztec Theater and Kennedy's new hotel wing.

Continuing on, one strolls past the 21-story Gothic-style Nix Hospital erected in 1930, and on by the former Riverside Hotel, whose upper floors have been converted to apartments while the lower floors contain restaurants and shops.

The north bank in this area has large cypress trees which may have been planted by the Herff family, well-known German immigrants, whose residence and gardens were located here.

The parking lot directly across the river from the Nix and the Riverside is to be developed into a 40,000 square foot com-

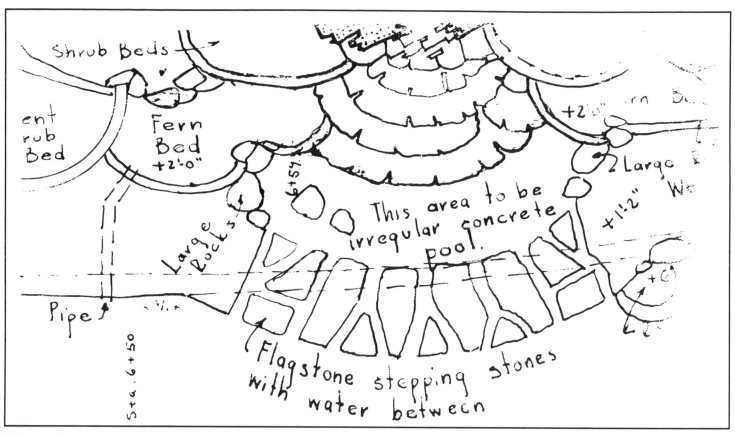

HUGMAN'S SKETCH OF NATURAL-LOOKING CHANNELS BETWEEN SIDEWALK PAVERS CARRYING WATER FROM A FOUNTAIN INTO THE RIVER.
Photo from Frank W. Phelps

HUGMAN'S UNIQUE STEPPING-STONE DRAINS ARE CROSSED EVERY DAY BY THOUSANDS OF PEOPLE PASSING LA MANSION DEL RIO HOTEL.
David Anthony Richelieu Photo

plex of restaurants and shops. A new footbridge spanning the river has been approved at this site.

The new South Bank complex has been designed so its three buildings reflect the scale and design of the many historic buildings in the immediate area.

A few steps further takes one to the site of a spring that was once a watering place for Indians and later for the early inhabitants of the Alamo. The site is marked by a plaque under the Presa Street Bridge.

Symbolic of the importance of water to San Antonio is a series of water sculptures and gardens connecting the River Walk to Alamo Plaza.

Designed by noted architect Boone Powell, the Paseo del Alamo symbolizes the dams, channels, aqueduct and acequias of the city's early water system. Water makes its way slowly through cascades, channels and falls that flow under Losoya Street and through the atrium/lobby of the Hyatt Regency Hotel.

The illusion is that the water flows from the lobby and out through slotted sidewalk channels and into the river. Actually, the water in the hotel is pumped back up to the top of the Paseo del Alamo and flows back down. The flow is stopped by a clear plastic panel under the Hyatt's glass wall. The pool on the outside with water lilies and other greenery is fed by a small pump that lets the water flow 15 feet or so across the sidewalk slots and back into the river.

This flow-through design is a modern interpretation of a small waterfall that Hugman designed that is in the block where La Mansion del Rio Hotel now stands. The terraced flower and water garden originally flowed with condensation runoff from the huge air-conditioning system at the Majestic Theater, which is directly across College Street from the site.

In Hugman's design, the water flows through grooves in the sidewalk between large pieces of natural flagstone.

And, perhaps symbolic of attitudes toward the river in recent decades, the trademark Hyatt atrium with its towering glass walls actually fronts on the River Walk rather than on the street.

The Hyatt Regency also houses a jazz band at a River Walk level club called the Landing. The band was one of the first to play on the River Walk and was once located in the basement of the Nix Hospital annex.

The Jim Cullum Jazz Band currently at the Landing has had a long association with the River Walk at various locations. The Landing is popular with tourists and local residents and jazz performances there are a regular nationally broadcast feature on public radio.

At the North Presa Street Bridge, the river turns abruptly south. Located across the water beyond the Crockett Street

Bridge is the six-story Casino Club Building constructed in 1927. It originally housed a German casino club organized in 1854. In 1981, the upper floors were converted to apartments and the lower floors became shops and restaurants.

South of the Casino Building is River Square, a complex of shops and restaurants fronting on two streets and along the River Walk.

It is usually filled with people enjoying food and drink under brightly colored umbrellas. Directly across, on the river's "sunny side," large cypress trees provide shady refuge for those sampling the outdoor restaurants or making their way to the shops on both river and street levels.

Buildings on both sides of the river formerly had their front doors facing the streets. But in the 1960's, owners converted the backs of the buildings to attractive riverside facades that are now their busiest entrances and where the prime dining and drinking areas are located. Some of the adjoining "turnaround" buildings have apartments as well as various jewelry, art, antique, folk art, clothing and other shops.

The atmosphere along this, the busiest section of the River Bend, is almost exactly as originally envisioned by Hugman in 1929.

The outdoor restaurants with serenading mariachis and iron-rail balconies on historic buildings exemplify the Old World flavor Hugman wanted along the River Walk.

The landscaping is diverse and beautiful. And the tempo matches that of Hugman's "lazy little river."

Strolling on, one encounters the aromas of different foods that tempt the palate. Mexican, Italian, Chinese, English, Texan, new Southwestern and other foods are offered along the stretch of river between Crockett and Commerce streets. Hugman's "Foods of the World" in Romula has become a reality for all to enjoy.

At the east end of the arched footbridge in this block is the five-story Losoya Building. It was constructed around 1908 and has been known as the Losoya, Hamilton, Talley, Milner and Paseo del Rio Hotels.

In 1980, its upper four floors were converted to luxury apartments. The street floor and basement now contain a restaurant/bar.

At street level south of the Losoya, a shop and restaurant occupy the site of the famous Original Mexican Food Restaurant founded by the O.M. Farnsworth family around 1900. In the 1980's, the name was resurrected on a restaurant directly across the river, but it has no real connection to the original Original.

Before World War II, one could buy a complete meal at the Original for 35 cents. Mr. Walter Schultze recalls that management required that all patrons be properly dressed. For anyone without a coat, a mohair one was provided. When its doors closed in 1960, it was the end of one of the oldest family-operated restaurants in the city. [56]

Across on the west bank by the Commerce Street Bridge stands the Clifford Building, with its distinctive round turret overlooking the crossing of the river and the street.

The four-story building with river-level basement was designed by James Riely Gordon in the Romanesque revival style popular when it was built in 1893 by Charles H. Clifford.

After the river beautification was completed in 1941, Hugman opened his office on the river in the Clifford Building. He purposely took river-level space to encourage others to establish commercial addresses on the river.

His former office space is now a restaurant, but the curved balcony face above the restaurant space has been restored as a marquee bearing Hugman's name exactly the way it looked when his office was there.

And, at river level, a plaque on the wall where Hugman had his office pays tribute to the genius and dedication of "The Father of the River Walk."

Street level of the Clifford contains shops, while the upper floors have been converted primarily to apartments.

The next bridge one passes under is the Commerce Street Bridge. In 1736, the first bridge across the San Antonio River was built here. Shortly before the Battle of the Alamo there were several confrontations over control of this crossing.

Defenders of the Alamo heard the chilling bugle call, "El Deguello," signalling "no quarter, utter destruction and no mercy" to the foe sounded from the west bank in this very area. The only disruptive element now heard is the frantic flutter of pigeons when they venture too close to the tables of outdoor diners at Casa Rio Mexican restaurant.

The Casa Rio building was built around 1898; its kitchen originally a dirt-floored basement often flooded by the river. The restaurant was opened in 1946 by A.F. Beyer and was the first establishment to serve food on the River Walk.

Descendants of Beyer, the William Lyons family, are current owners and operators. Lyons also holds the city contract to operate the fleet of 36 passenger and dining barges on the river — although guests can have food served on board by whatever restaurant they choose.

Continuing on, one climbs the arched footbridge built to cross a man-made river extension built in 1968.

This channel passes under what is now Convention Plaza where Losoya, Alamo and Commerce streets converge then makes its way past the Greater San Antonio Chamber of Commerce Building.

The right branch of the channel curves past a Marriott Hotel, under Market Street and ends in a lagoon in the middle of

STONE AND METAL FRAMEWORK OF RIVERCENTER RISES AROUND THE CITY-BUILT RIVER LAGOON THAT SERVES AS THE MALL'S CENTERPIECE.

LOOKING FROM THE COMMERCE STREET BRIDGE OVER THE NEW RIVER EXTENSION TO RIVERCENTER MALL SHOWS CONSTRUCTION OF THE MAIN ENTRANCE AND THE 'MARKET BRIDGE' GATEWAY TO THE MALL'S 120 STORES AND SHOPS. *Rivercenter mall Photos*

THIS IS HOW THE 'HILTON' BEND IN THE RIVER, JUST UPSTREAM FROM THE ARNESON RIVER THEATER, LOOKED BEFORE HEMISFAIR '68.
San Antonio Conservation Society Photo

A NEW ARCHED BRIDGE HELPED RIVER WALK STROLLERS GET PAST THE SITE OF THE HILTON HOTEL DEMOLITION AND CONSTRUCTION.
San Antonio Light Photo

AS CONSTRUCTION OF THE HILTON PALACIO DEL RIO HOTEL HURRIES ALONG TO OPEN IN TIME FOR HEMISFAIR '68, THE COMPLETELY FURNISHED CONCRETE MODULAR ROOMS ARE STACKED IN PLACE BY CRANE, SETTING A WORLD RECORD FOR MAJOR HOTEL CONSTRUCTION.
San Antonio Light Photo

the Convention Center, which was built for HemisFair. A new branch of the same channel veers left at the Marriott Hotel and goes under Commerce Street to Rivercenter mall, which has an attached 40-story, 1,000-room hotel, also a Marriott.

Rivercenter was completed in 1988 and has three levels, beginning with a river-level food court, stores and restaurants and a variety of shops, a comedy club, a nine-screen movie complex and an IMAX theater with a six-story screen.

The lagoon in the center of the U-shaped mall has a small bridged entertainment island for staging shows, such as the annual Christmas pageant.

The design of this newer extension channel follows ideas Hugman used in the River Bend, though high rock walls were necessary because of the topography of the area.

There is a variety of plants, a waterfall and several foot bridges crossing the river, but there is no commercial frontage until one reaches Rivercenter by walking under a arched steel truss bridge the city built on Commerce Street to link the mall to the river extension.

Returning down the extension toward the River Bend and continuing south under the Market Street Bridge, one hears the bustle of an Irish pub and encounters a group of tables on the walk by the Hilton Palacio del Rio Hotel.

This 400-room hotel was completed in a record 202 working days between July 6, 1967, and March 8, 1968, using a modular construction technique perfected by the H.B. Zachry Co.

Each box-like room was of cast steel-reinforced concrete. All plumbing and wiring were installed, the glass wall and doors, balcony railing, all the carpet, furnishings, bathroom fixtures and other trim, even the swag lamps, were all installed at the Zachry plant on the South Side of town.

Each fully furnished room was then lifted by crane and placed on a low-boy tractor-trailer that hauled it to the hotel site. There, another crane connected cables to steel lifting loops built into the top corners of the room. A small fan on a triangular brace and powered by a car battery was bolted to the rear of the room to prevent it from spinning when the crane pulled it up and stacked it in place.

Once each room was precisely settled, crews connected it to the main utility lines. During the construction process, only one room was damaged and had to be taken back for repairs.

Nestled next to the Hilton, where the river abruptly turns west, is the Bombach house constructed about 1855.

The building has been known as Conservation Corner since being purchased in 1950 by the San Antonio Conservation Society, which leased it to a restaurateur.

It had once been a home, boarding house, German beer hall, gambling salon, a hangout for desperados and a small museum.

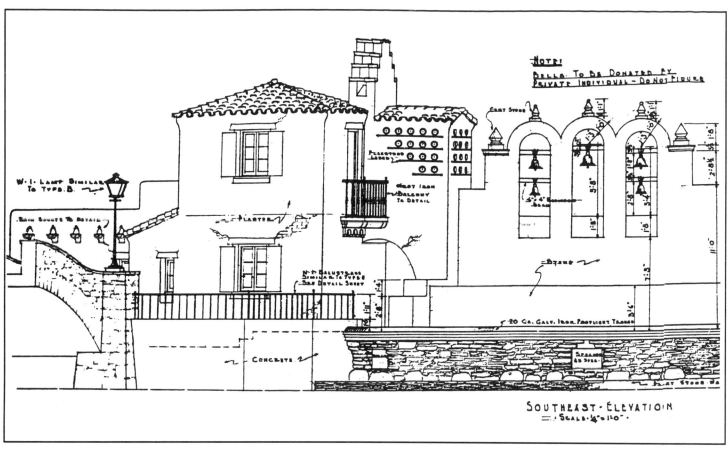

DRAWING OF THE STAGE, STAGEHOUSE AND STONE ARCHES FROM HUGMAN'S PLANS FOR THE BROADCAST THEATER REVEALS HIS ATTENTION TO DETAIL. HUGMAN HAD THE THEATER NAMED IN HONOR OF ENGINEER ED ARNESON, WHO DIED BEFORE THE CONSTRUCTION BEGAN.

CONSTRUCTION OF THE ARNESON RIVER THEATER SHOWS THE STAGE EXTENDING OUT INTO THE RIVER CHANNEL AND THE STONE ARCHED BRIDGE CONNECTING THE AUDIENCE AND STAGE SIDES OF THE THEATER THAT ARE LOCATED ON OPPOSITE BANKS OF THE STREAM.
San Antonio Light Photo

The attractive rock structure was one of the first two-story buildings in San Antonio. Its contrast with its towering contemporary neighbor is a reminder that commercial development can be effectively accomplished without destroying the significance of historic buildings lining the river.

The next building in which a restaurant is housed was the last private dwelling in La Villita (the little town site whose early huts were probably built in the early 1700's). Purchased in 1970 by the Frank W. Phelps family, it was turned into a gourmet restaurant called the Fig Tree.

Next door is the Dashiel House, built in 1850 and restored in 1942 by the San Antonio Conservation Society. This building now houses the offices for "A Night in Old San Antonio," a four-day celebration of food and music during San Antonio's annual Fiesta. NIOSA, sponsored by the Conservation Society and held in La Villita, is one of Fiesta's most popular events.

A plaque on the retaining wall for the NIOSA office honors Hugman for his contributions to the River Walk.

Next, one sees the curved terraces of seats of the Arneson River Theater that were literally carved out of the river bank and whose sitting areas are grass. The Arneson was built in an area that in the 1930's was used for storing machine and auto parts.

Across the river from the seats is the stage of the Arneson with its backdrop of three stone arches, and adjacent tile-roofed house with dressing rooms and other support space. A small stone bridge connects the audience side to the stage side of the theater. During performances, barges glide by in the river right between the audience and the entertainers.

The Arneson was originally named the Broadcast Theater, envisioned as the home of live radio musical, drama and other entertainment shows. The Arneson has seen many different events, from rock and country music concerts to Mexican folkloric dance revues to religious sunrise services and nationally televised talk shows, political debates and interviews.

One of the most-spectacular productions ever seen on the Arneson stage was the San Antonio Festival's fully staged presentation of Bizet's opera, "Carmen," in 1984. It featured the conductor and soloists of the Berlin Opera, with music performed by San Antonio Symphony members who were seated in floating barges anchored to the front of the stage.

Atop the Arneson stairs adjacent to the entry is the Cos House where, on December 10, 1835, Mexican Gen. Martin Perfecto de Cos signed the terms of surrender after a battle against a small force of Texans that had been led by Ben Milam, who was killed in the assault.

The "Cos House" had once been the home of Maria Rafaela Martinez, daughter of Antonio Martinez, the last Spanish Governor of Texas.

Beyond the Arneson River Theater there is little commercial presence on the river. This area is very serene and park-like, containing benches and lush greenery.

The contrast between this area and the commercial stretch of the River Walk between the Hyatt Regency and the Arneson River Theater exemplifies the diversity that Hugman had emphasized.

His objective of having the river accommodate both commercial activities and park-like natural settings has been achieved and is being maintained through a careful balancing of interests. But a growing number of proposed projects and expansions of existing commercial establishments may threaten this balance in the future.

At the South Presa Street Bridge, a tiny island is linked to the walk by a small arched footbridge.

This was once the site of the dam that diverted water down the acequia to Mission Concepcion. It is also where a dam was built for the Nat Lewis Mill that opened in 1847 on the north bank close to the Navarro Street Bridge. Before the mill was built, the location was a popular river crossing — a fact noted in a tile mural on the north wall.

The gracefully arched Navarro Street Bridge recalls Paris' elegant Pont Neuf across the Seine.

Strolling due west, one can see the base of the Tower Life Building, formerly known as the Smith-Young Tower and, later, as the Transit Tower.

Built in 1929, the 29-story Perpendicular Gothic-style sky-scraper was the tallest building west of Chicago. For more than 50 years, it was the tallest building in San Antonio. The building stands in the old river bed. Until the 1920's, the area was called Bowen's Island, which was actually a series of irregular peninsulas that became a popular entertainment center for swimming, circuses and rodeos.

At the end of the River Bend near the Granada Apartments (the former Plaza Hotel), one can climb the steps that cross over the flood gates.

These flood gates were installed in the early 1970's and replaced a beautiful curved waterfall that was one of Hugman's outstanding design and engineering features. What stood at this south end of the River Bend was a gracefully curved dam that maintained an even water level in the bend area and also assured that the water through the bend would still flow and not stagnate.

The "horseshoe falls" were especially liked by Hugman because they kept water movement in the River Bend calm and peaceful.

Turk, however, saw them differently -- as a construction challenge, since the lip of the dam had to be perfectly level to

BEAUTIFUL HORSESHOE FALLS WAS HUGMAN'S SOUTH TERMINUS OF THE RIVER WALK. THE EVEN FLOW SEEN ACROSS THE RIM WAS ACHIEVED THROUGH CAREFUL HAND-HONING OF THE LIP. THE FALLS, HOWEVER, WERE REMOVED IN A LATER CHANNEL MODIFICATION.
San Antonio Conservation Society Photo

PERFORMANCES UNDER THE STARS ARE TRANSFORMED BY THE SPECTACULAR AND UNIQUE SETTING OF THE ARNESON RIVER THEATER.
Texas Highways Magazine

CHRISTMAS PAGEANT IN THE LAGOON OF RIVERCENTER MALL IS AMONG DAZZLING ANNUAL HOLIDAY SPECTACLES ON THE RIVER WALK.
Rivercenter mall Photo

COLORFUL CULTURAL TRADITIONS FROM **300** YEARS OF HISTORY THRIVE ALONG THE RIVER THAT REMAINS THE HEART OF SAN ANTONIO.
Texas Highways Magazine

NATURAL BEAUTY IN THE MIDDLE OF DOWNTOWN WAS AN ESSENTIAL ELEMENT OF HUGMAN'S DREAM AND VISION OF THE RIVER WALK.
Texas Highways Magazine

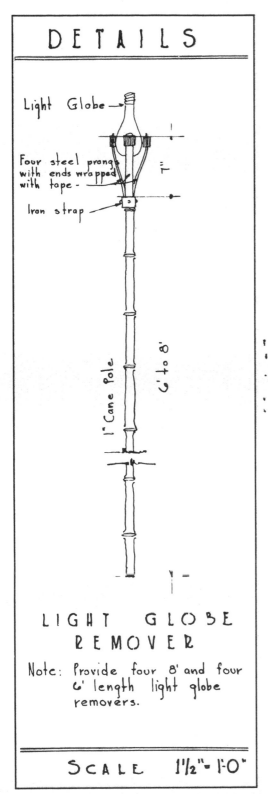

DETAILS

Light Globe

Four steel prongs with ends wrapped with tape -

Iron strap

1" Cane Pole

6' to 8'

LIGHT GLOBE REMOVER

Note: Provide four 8' and four 6' length light globe removers.

SCALE 1½"= 1'-0"

INGENIOUS LIGHT-BULB CHANGER SHOWS THE EXTENSIVE DETAIL WORK IN HUGMAN'S PLAN.

allow the water to flow evenly over the entire face of the structure. Turk said that it had taken several individuals many hours of painstaking work to hand hone the top edge of the dam to achieve the proper waterfall flow.

The waterfall disappeared when a new dam was constructed downstream in the main channel, raising the channel's water level up to the same level as that of the River Bend.

There were 31 stairways constructed during the WPA work on the river. No two are exactly alike.

While Hugman emphasized diversity in the elements along the River Walk, he also quite ingeniously maintained a sense of unity with a coherent design vocabulary tying the entire project together.

The arched opening of his south gate structure was built without steel reinforcement. Stone was quarried near Brackenridge Park and cut according to specifications to form a Roman arch-like structure.

From our vantage point in the 1990's, it is not difficult to see Hugman's design for the River Walk as a total concept similar to today's planned communities or even theme parks.

A close examination of Hugman's original plans and blueprints reveals he anticipated even the smallest details of the project, right down to a bamboo pole with tape-wrapped prongs for removing bulbs from the light fixtures along the River Walk.

But in the late 1920's, few fully understood or shared the perspective evident in Hugman's creative and well-coordinated design scheme.

The River Walk plan succeeds marvelously because it deliberately avoids looking as if it is all formally coordinated. This same design philosophy guided Frederick Olmsted's plan for Central Park in New York City which was not natural at all, but was brilliantly designed to look that way.

The vision of Hugman's plan for the River Walk was just as remarkable. It was so far ahead of its time that, for two decades after its construction, some insisted people would never want to be on the River Walk. So, the fully constructed River Walk just sat there in the middle of a city that didn't quite know what to do with it.

At least it was only ignored and not damaged or destroyed.

Then in the 1960's, San Antonio rediscovered its River Walk — and the rest of the world hasn't been far behind.

Now, the Paseo del Rio is being recognized as the masterpiece of urban design it really is.

On our stroll we have seen both the natural and commercial faces and moods of the River Walk.

There is the Old World charm Hugman infused into the Paseo del Rio. There is unrivalled beauty, epic history, commercial use and places where people live along its banks.

Hugman's flair for romantic Old World design on the river is exemplified by the Arneson River Theater stage house.
Ruben Alfaro Photo

The arched stone bridge joining the River Bend to the main channel was just behind Hugman's now-gone waterfalls.
San Antonio Express-News Photo

This, indeed, was Hugman's concept for the development of the River Walk that he had envisioned back in the 1920's.

On July 24, 1980, an editorial appeared in the San Antonio Express entitled "Paseo del Rio's Architect Left a Distinct Monument."

Excerpts from this editorial are a meaningful reminder of the legacy Hugman left to the city of his birth and to everyone who strolls the River Walk today:

"The architect whose design and hard work resulted in Paseo del Rio years later, died this week at age 78, having seen his dream realized and, belatedly, had the satisfaction of public recognition for the achievement . . . .

"His dream has been solidly vindicated. His foresight and determination literally gave San Antonio its center-city gem — Paseo del Rio."

THIS DECEPTIVELY SERENE STRETCH OF RIVER FROM PRESA STREET WEST TOWARD NAVARRO STREET IS ALREADY ONE OF THE LIVELIEST AREAS ON THE RIVER. THE NEW SOUTH BANK DEVELOPMENT PLANNED AT THE LEFT IN THIS PICTURE WILL ADD EVEN MORE ACTIVITY.

Ruben Alfaro Photo

CHAPTER ELEVEN

The River Walk Of the Future

The memories of the San Antonio River that span more than 300 years of recorded history and the colorful development of the River Walk manifest an Old World charm that is uniquely San Antonio's.

Visitors have stated over and over again that they not only recognize the romantic atmosphere here but also sense something different and unique.

This enthusiasm for something different is understandable when cities are continually being referred to as "look-a-likes." While San Antonio has its share of the ordinary, it also has something quite special — a River Walk that is recognized as a world-class masterpiece of urban design.

The San Antonio River Walk is a priceless inheritance because it has been properly nurtured.

In April of 1982, a national committee of the American Institute of Architects urged the City of San Antonio to adopt design controls for the River Walk and its environs.

They argued that extensions and additions to the River Walk must be maintained as "America's finest example of urban design."

And a resolution by the committee supported "public design controls that will insure that new development preserves the intimate scale and sunlight of the river and that the new buildings are compatible in character and, above all, in scale with the older buildings that contribute so much to the city's charm and success."[57]

While the River Walk can be described, the magical allure of its special atmosphere and ambience cannot be fully captured by mere words.

But the AIA committee of architects from across the country readily sensed and appreciated what Hugman had achieved in his design plan for the River Walk.

Their recommendations must be heeded if development is to be successfully extended north and south of the busy River Bend area once the few choice parcels of available land are gone.

Maintaining a balance between commercial interests and green space is essential to the River Walk's future. Perhaps it is time to plant more bougainvillea instead of setting up another table for two.

It is just as important to control and monitor events and activities on the River Walk.

An example of compatible development on the river has been the beautification of what had been built only as a utilitarian concrete-walled flood channel south of downtown through the King William Historic District or "Old German Town."

A cooperative effort between the City of San Antonio and the San Antonio River Authority — organized in 1937 by the State Legislature — and the U.S. Army Corps of Engineers, resulted in two River Walk additions very similar in scale and design to Hugman's original linear park design.

SCENE LOOKING NORTH TOWARD THE TOWER LIFE BUILDING SHOWS HOW THE RIVER CHANNEL LOOKED BEFORE RECENT IMPROVEMENTS.
The Institute of Texan Cultures

RIVER BEAUTIFICATION WORK EXTENDED THE RIVER WALK AMBIENCE SOUTH OF DOWNTOWN TO THE HISTORIC KING WILLIAM DISTRICT.
David Anthony Richelieu Photo

The first extension, from South Alamo Street to Arsenal Street, was completed in 1984 and the second section, from Arsenal to Durango Boulevard, was finished in 1987.

Since this is primarily a residential area, the improvements create a park-like atmosphere where there originally were sheer walls designed only for flood and erosion control. Most of the new plantings are low-maintenance shrubs, flowers and trees.

These improvements helped attract the headquarters of one of the state's largest grocery firms not just to San Antonio, but to downtown, and on the river where the historic U.S. Arsenal complex was restored and renovated into corporate offices. The H.E.B. Grocery headquarters sits atop an expansive slope of grassed flood channel and the landscaping visibly extends through the ornamental iron fences surrounding the company compound.

One can now stroll from the heart of downtown to King William and experience many of the same delights that were designed into the River Bend more than 50 years ago.

MANAGING THE RIVER WALK

The San Antonio Parks and Recreation Department is responsible for the maintenance of the River Walk and its extensions north and south on the main river channel.

The river and its banks are city park land.

The widened flood control drainage channels south of downtown are under the supervision of the San Antonio River Authority. The River Authority and the U.S. Army Corps of Engineers have jurisdiction over all river-related construction or improvements to determine that they will not adversely affect water flow during heavy rain runoff.

Planning for public amenities along the river is done by the Parks Department and the River Authority. Both agencies have jurisdiction to review any and all privately financed developments fronting on the river.

Review of projects planned along the river is done by the Historic and Design Review Commission, an advisory body to City Council staffed by the City Planning Department. The entire river within the city limits is an official City of San Antonio Historical Landmark.

The Parks Department also receives recommendations from the Parks and Recreation Advisory Commission and is aided by the San Antonio Parks Foundation in park projects throughout the city.

The River Authority's planning is done with advice from the River Corridor Advisory Committee as well as from the regional inter-governmental agency, the Alamo Area Council of Governments.

The Parks Department has more than 50 people assigned full time to River Walk maintenance, security and operations, including the raising and lowering of the seven flood gates during heavy runoff to seal off the River Bend and release high

MAJOR HOTELS LIKE THE HILTON PALACIO DEL RIO SEEN HERE GIVE EVIDENCE OF THE SUCCESS OF HUGMAN'S VISION OF THE RIVER WALK AS A NATURAL-LOOKING SETTING THAT WOULD HELP PROMOTE COMMERCIAL DEVELOPMENT AND BOOST TOURISM.
Ruben Alfaro Photo

TOURISTS IN A BARGE GLIDE UNDER GIANT CYPRESS TREES TOWERING ABOVE THE RIVER WALK NEAR THE NAVARRO STREET BRIDGE.
David Anthony Richelieu Photo

water from the main channel. Parks personnel took over flood-gate duties from the Fire Department in 1993.

There is an 80-person force of Park Rangers whose members patrol the River Walk 24 hours a day on foot and in river patrol boats. San Antonio Police, who have a downtown foot and bike patrol substation a short city block from the River Walk also have enforcement and patrol jurisdiction on the river.

The River Walk is lined with tropical shrubberies such as hibiscus, bougainvillea, plumbago, philodendron, croton and cycad. Joining the tropicals are hardier shrubs such as Indian Hawthorn, holly, mahonia, Lady Banksia rose and pyracantha.

In fact, there are more than 400 kinds of shrubbery on the River Walk. More than 30 people carry out two major plantings of more than 30,000 annuals each year.

In the fall, petunia, pansy, dianthus, snapdragon, alyssum and dahlia are planted and in late spring marigold, salvia, zinnia, coreopsis ageratum and coleus. About 50 new trees a year are planted to replace those lost to old age, disease, damage or frost.

In 1962, business leader David Straus framed an ordinance establishing the River Walk Advisory Commission which operated under the Parks Department.

This commission was empowered to review all building projects along the river and to enforce and enact policies on leasing, signage, noise, types of business and any and all changes and improvements planned in the River Bend and the river extensions.[58]

Two other city advisory boards whose jurisdictions extended to the River Walk were formed in the ensuing years.

The Historic Review Board was created to protect San Antonio's vast inventory of historic districts and landmarks. The city passed the state's first historic protection ordinance, created 10 historic districts, eventually inventoried and recognized as historic landmarks some 1,300 individual buildings and sites in the downtown area.

It was this board that declared the San Antonio River, from its headwaters to the southern city limits, a city historic landmark.

The Fine Arts Commission was charged with jurisdiction over projects built by the city or built on city land, including the River Walk, since it is a city park.

In late 1992, the city consolidated the functions of the three advisory agencies whose overlapping jurisdictions caused developers to complain of having to go back and forth between these groups for approval of proposed projects.

The combined powers of the River Walk Advisory Commission, the Historic Review Board and the Fine Arts Commission was given to a new City Historic and Design Review Commission and it was placed under the City Planning Department for staffing and funding purposes.

RESTAURANTS ABOUND ALONG THE STRETCH OF RIVER WALK HUGMAN ENVISIONED AS AN AREA CALLED THE FOODS OF ALL NATIONS.
David Anthony Richelieu Photo

The future development of the River Walk has not only been the concern of business owners and developers but also of many other citizens.

In 1963, the Paseo del Rio Association, a private organization of River Walk property owners and business operators, was organized to assume responsibility of leading the way in further commercial development and promotion of the river. The association continues to function with a director and staff that publishes a monthly newsletter and sponsors or coordinates various festivals and special events along the river.

Columns appear frequently in the newspaper on heated debates over new proposals along the River Walk. Business leaders are interviewed about conceptual plans and it is not unusual to find discussions among River Walk residents about the latest news of key decisions that could affect the river's environs and its future.

There is growing concern among citizens for city government to take stronger measures to control and encourage development of properties along the River Walk and adjacent areas at street level.

For example, there should be incentives to encourage the reconditioning of empty buildings into apartment complexes for more downtown residents and/or office complexes for business organizations. Other amenities could include playgrounds and parks, development of outlet stores, and recognizable boundaries that define historic districts and landmarks.

THE NEW TUNNELS

The San Antonio River has a long history of flooding the downtown area. In fact, the city recorded 15 major floods between 1819 and 1913.

As a result, the city hired Metcalf & Eddy engineering firm to propose flood-control solutions. The report was completed in December 1920, just months before the disastrous flood of 1921.

Among their recommendations were the construction of Olmos Dam and straightening and widening the river and some of its tributaries. Since the 1920's, many of the recommendations were implemented. However, the threat of flooding and the emphasis on flood control has continued to be a major issue for the city, especially after a severe flood in 1946.

Several flood control studies since then have focused on two basic options. One was to excavate the river channel much deeper and wider, line the river bottom with concrete and line most of the river channel with 30-foot deep retaining walls. This costly option also would have required removal of virtually all the historic concrete, steel and iron bridges in downtown to have them replaced with wider and longer new bridges to span the widened river channel.

Fortunately, this plan was rejected, thanks to opposition from the city's design-review advisory boards and others

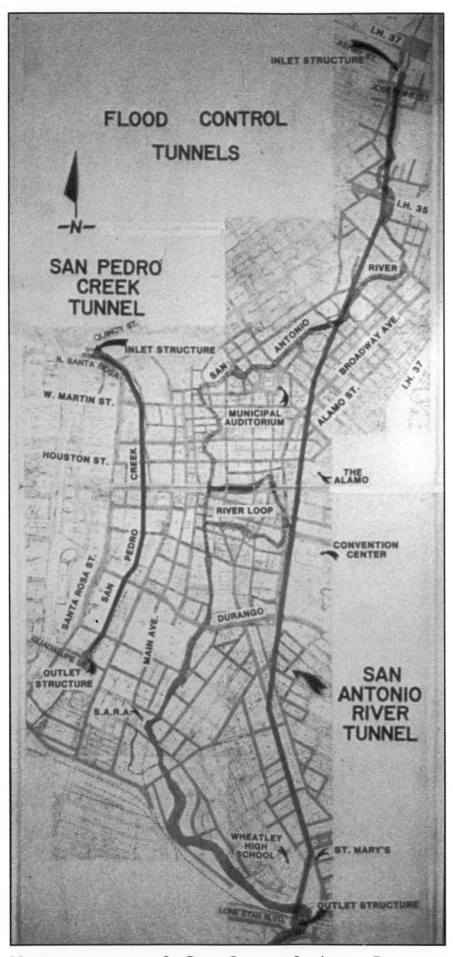

MAP SHOWS ROUTES OF THE SAN PEDRO CREEK AND SAN ANTONIO RIVER FLOOD CONTROL TUNNELS UNDER DOWNTOWN. *U.S. Army Corps of Engineers Photo*

alarmed about its potential negative impact on downtown, the river and the River Walk.

The second option, which was the one ultimately adopted, proposed constructing two diversion tunnels approximately 140 to 150 feet underground that would carry excessive runoff from the San Pedro Creek basin and the San Antonio River channel under the downtown area and directly to the widened flood channel already built along the river route on the city's South Side.

Both tunnels are in place and the San Pedro Creek tunnel is operational. The San Antonio River channel is expected to be operational in 1996.

The inverted-siphon tunnels were designed for a dual purpose. Their primary purpose is to take heavy rain runoff from north of downtown and divert it under the city to the widened flood channel south of Lone Star Brewery.

Secondly, the San Antonio River tunnel will always be full of water in order to operate as a siphon. Reverse-flow pumps are being installed to recycle all the water normally in the river and pump it back up to the inlet tunnel south of Brackenridge Park, then let the water run down the river again through downtown. The pumps can recycle all the water in the river, but are then operated in normal mode when high water flows into the river channel.

Excavation for the San Pedro Creek tunnel began in November, 1988 and was completed in July 1989. The tunnel became operational in June 1991. It is approximately 5,843 feet long and 24 feet, 4 inches in diameter and is at a depth of 140 feet. It begins at an inlet shaft downstream of Quincy Street and extends to an outlet shaft near Guadalupe Street. It also contains inlet and outlet structures that are pear-shaped. For example, the San Pedro Creek outlet structure is 207 feet across the opening and gradually narrows to the diameter of the tunnel.

An 18-foot-diameter maintenance shaft has been installed between Travis and Houston streets. Other ventilation and instrumentation shafts have been installed. The tunnel can store approximately 22 million gallons of water. This tunnel cost $12,749,426.

The San Antonio River tunnel is 16,082 feet long with an inside diameter of 24 feet 4 inches and is approximately 150 feet below the surface. This tunnel starts near Josephine Street just south of Brackenridge Park and ends north of Lone Star Boulevard.

South of Brooklyn Avenue, the tunnel passes under several commercial and industrial structures, the largest being the 15-story Valero Energy Building at Avenue B and McCullough Avenue.

As the tunnel continues south, it follows the alignment of South Alamo street through downtown and passes under Alamo Plaza and on past HemisFair Park, the 20-story Hilton Hotel, La Villita and the Plaza San Antonio Hotel.

WORKMEN STAND NEXT TO THE GIANT BORING MACHINE USED TO DRILL THE SAN ANTONIO RIVER FLOOD TUNNEL TO CARRY FLOOD RUNOFF UNDER DOWNTOWN TO PROTECT THE CITY CENTER AND THE RIVER WALK. *U.S. Army Corps of Engineers Photo*

THE SCENE INSIDE THE BORED-OUT SAN ANTONIO RIVER FLOOD TUNNEL UNDER DOWNTOWN SHOWS THE SMALL TRAIN USED TO HAUL DIRT REMOVED BY THE BORING MACHINE TO THE ACCESS SHAFT AND THEN TO THE SURFACE. *U.S. Army Corps of Engineers Photo*

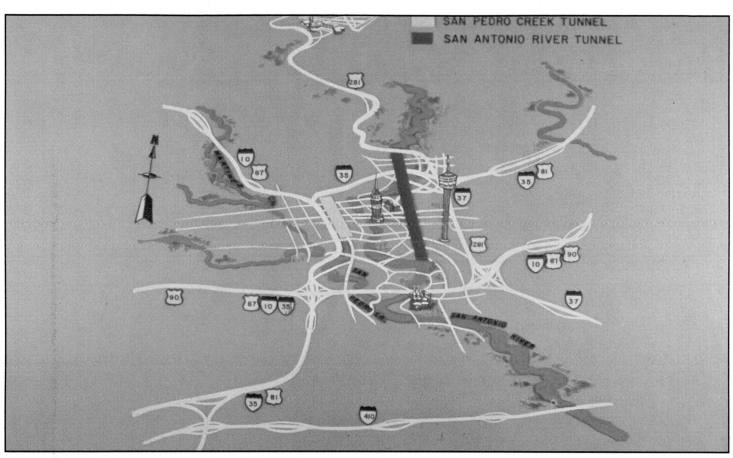

AERIAL VIEW OF SAN ANTONIO FROM THE SOUTH SHOWS ROUTES OF SAN PEDRO CREEK AND SAN ANTONIO RIVER FLOOD TUNNELS.

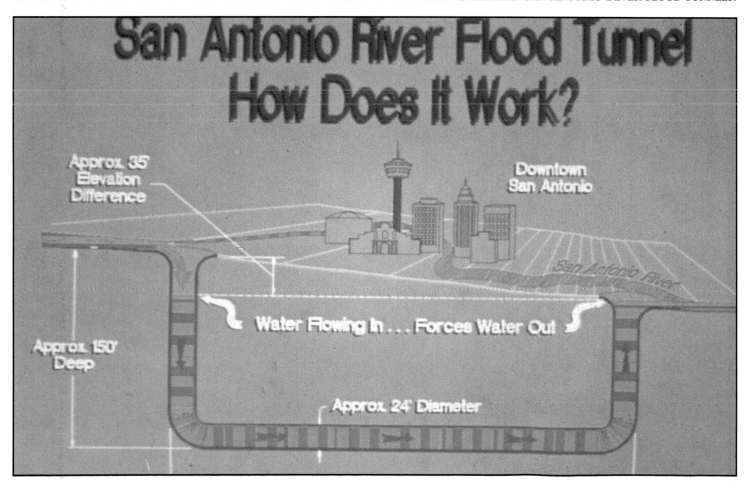

CROSS-SECTION EAST THROUGH DOWNTOWN SHOWS HOW THE SAN ANTONIO RIVER FLOOD TUNNEL DIVERTS RUNOFF FROM NEAR BRACKENRIDGE PARK, LEFT, UNDER THE CITY TO THE OUTLET NEAR LONE STAR BREWERY. *San Antonio River Authority Drawings*

DINING IN SHIMMERING TWILIGHT ALONG THE SAN ANTONIO RIVER IS PART OF THE INCREDIBLE LEGACY LEFT THE CITY BY RIVER WALK ARCHITECT ROBERT H.H. HUGMAN.
Texas Highways Magazine

Finally, the tunnel turns and follows along under South St. Mary's Street to the Eagleland Drive intersection where it turns west to the river. The tunnel outlet structure is south of the Southern Pacific Railroad spur on the west bank of the river. Like the other tunnel, it also has maintenance and ventilation shafts. This tunnel can store approximately 58 million gallons of water.

The original contract cost for both tunnels was $35,090,924, but difficulties encountered while boring the river tunnel eventually raised the cost to $54,090,924.

Excavators crossed two geological formations. The Navarro formation was in the first 2,000 feet while the remaining length of tunnel went through the Taylor formation. Progress went well until February, 1990, when large fallout cavities developed in front and above the tunnel boring machine. The Navarro rock formation was described as containing high angle joints and fractures with horizontal sand seams. When the tunnel boring machine excavated the rock, large chunks of rock collapsed, hampering forward progress.

After several "fallout chambers" developed, the Corps of Engineers decided to excavate a temporary shaft on Brackenridge High School property to intersect the tunnel alignment. The shaft was located in a fault that separated the Navarro and Taylor formations. The top half of the tunnel was excavated and stabilized until it reached the boring machine, which was stuck directly under the girls' gym of the high school.

Once it was freed, the boring machine then continued with excavating the bottom half of the tunnel through the rest of the Navarro formation — a task that added more than a year to the work schedule. The inlet structure for the San Antonio River tunnel has a sloped apron to direct water into a 25-foot diameter vertical shaft down to the main tunnel. Both the inlet and outlet structures will feature amenities such as water fountains and extensive greenery.

These tunnels should have a major impact on flood control since they were designed to handle half the runoff of the worst-known flood in the past 100 years. The other half of the 100-year flood waters can be handled within the existing banks of the downtown river.

Because the tunnel can recycle the water in the downtown river, it will help ease demand for water from the Edwards aquifer. With the tunnel pumps, it will no longer be necessary for the city to pump the average 5 millions per day now needed to maintain proper flow and water levels in the downtown sections of the river.

The San Antonio Water System also plans to run a 36-inch pipe from its Dos Rios treatment plant south of the city to carry fully treated sewage water up to the inlet tunnel to be used in place of any fresh aquifer water.

Completion of the river tunnel will also make it possible to plan new developments along stretches of the river north of the downtown River Bend. By controlling excessive water during and after heavy rains, the tunnel will reduce potential damage that has discouraged development near river level in areas north of downtown.

The map on Page 184 shows the tunnel routes do not follow straight lines. The San Pedro Creek tunnel follows the creek bed while the San Antonio River tunnel follows city streets as much as possible. The routes were chosen because of a state law that requires property owners be paid for the use of their land even though the tunnels are 140 to 150 feet below the surface.

Excavation work was done by a Japanese firm with an American-built machine. The machine is seen on Page 186.

The borer face rotated, causing the disc cutters to fracture the rock while depositing excavated material on a conveyer belt that emptied into small train cars carrying the rock to a hoist at the outlet shaft where it was lifted to the surface and hauled off by truck. The machine was driven by very large and powerful electric motors.[59]

FUTURE PLANS FOR THE RIVER

In addition to flood control, the most recent plans for the San Antonio River have centered around enhanced economic development, creating recreational opportunities and improving the appearance of the river channel in areas outside of the River Bend area.

In September 1988, a study of the river corridor south of downtown was undertaken as a cooperative effort of the City of San Antonio, San Antonio River Authority, National Park Service, Bexar County and selected consultants.

The study area extended from Guenther Street in the King William District south to Espada Park. This area includes the San Antonio Missions National Historical Park, part of the King William Historic District, Mission Historic District, the San Antonio River Corridor and several older inner-city riverside neighborhoods.

This South Study included extensive evaluations of current land use, existing site conditions, environmental requirements, aesthetic improvements, maintenance, security, and zoning and governing entities. Public input was obtained at a series of 70 meetings. The result was a conceptual plan for new and improved hike/bike paths, new trees, native grasses and wildflowers, river overlook areas, establishing an island for wildlife habitat, and building a parkway thoroughfare.

Other issues included channel stabilization, erosion control measures, building of small dams, silt removal and flood control methods. Also proposed is a connection linking the proposed hike trails in the river channel with the existing River Walk through King William to downtown. The connection would be a cantilevered walk along the concrete river channel wall near the Alamo Street Bridge in King William. Also included are plans for walkways on both sides of the river channel where possible. Pedestrian crossing areas will be at small dams and there would be connections from the walkways to parks that are near or adjacent to the river channel.

The South Study was completed in early 1993. Estimated cost of the project was $40 million to $50 million, and additional options, such as the San Juan Channel Dam replacement, right-of-way improvements and construction of a parkway would add another $24 million for a total of nearly $75 million. The city had no immediate plans to fund the proposed improvements.

Two additional studies, titled the North Study, cover the San Antonio river channel north of Nueva Street to Brackenridge Park near the river's headwaters.

The first North Study, completed in the fall of 1993, covers Nueva Street to the McAllister Freeway on the southern edge of Brackenridge Park. The second North Study from the McAllister to the headwaters is to begin shortly.

Cost estimates for improvements from Nueva Street to the McAllister Freeway run over $72 million, with another $9.8 million for a dam at Brooklyn Avenue. The same approach and systematic procedures of the South Study were used in the first of the north studies.

Design recommendations from Nueva to Villita Street include continuous walkways along both sides of the channel to make an uninterrupted connection along the entire length of the River Walk. A continuous walk exists on the east bank all the way from King William up to Lexington Avenue near the Municipal Auditorium. But there are several breaks in the route on the west bank. The new study proposes filling in all the gaps with cantilevered or surface walks where none presently exists.

Also proposed is a major pedestrian connection from the River Walk up to Main Plaza. This plan envisions a terraced stairway down to the River Walk where a barge landing would be built. Pedestrians and barge riders can take elevators or wide terraced stairs up to the historic City Center area that includes Main Plaza, San Fernando Cathedral, the Spanish Governor's Palace, Bexar County Courthouse and City Hall.

Upstream from where the River Walk ends at Lexington Avenue, a dam is planned between McCullough and Brooklyn Avenues to create a navigable pool of water at a level 10 feet higher than in the present River Walk channel.

The dam would allow water to back up near the San Antonio Museum of Art and other stops to the north where river barges could bring passengers from the downtown area.

Two major objectives in the North Channel study were the creation of a continuous walkway and allowing river barge access from downtown up to the new river tunnel inlet near Josephine Street and the McAllister Freeway.

While both goals are attainable, river barge travel from downtown will involve a brief transfer from one barge to another where the river water level will change behind the new

Brooklyn Avenue dam. The north River Walk extension proposal also includes the construction of four pedestrian bridges across the river, one railroad bridge, several stairwells from the river to street level, and an island.

Throughout the study report, there are repeated references to Hugman's historic design features and a recommendation that "the Hugman style will be duplicated to preserve continuity between different sections of the River Walk." Also the original components of Hugman walls and sidewalks are to be salvaged and incorporated into the renovated walkways.

A most encouraging position taken by the groups involved in the planning process for further development of the river is the historical land use of the target areas. The study emphasizes not only the pragmatic use of the river but recognizes the significance of the river's rich history.

There appears to be a keen awareness of the need for architecture, scale and design elements that complement the existing River Walk created from Hugman's original concept.[60]

The second North Study will begin in 1994 with a series of public meetings on planned improvements from the McAllister Freeway north through Brackenridge Park. The hearings will help determine whether the far north section should be developed similar to the rest of the North Channel or left in a more natural state.

However, these recently developed conceptual plans do not guarantee that the current River Walk theme will be continued in the future. Plans can be changed for a variety of reasons, including business and personal interests.

Although some diversity of design in the north and south proposed extensions may be dictated by terrain and topography, it is important that planning continues to focus on the charm of the river as the stage for all of its future settings. Such a focus requires that future development be cognizant of Old World eclectic architecture that brought cohesion to Hugman's original model.

New buildings, plazas, walkways and stairwells should be in scale and compatible in character with what has made the River Walk a world masterpiece of urban design.

It is most essential that citizens and organized groups monitor future river plans, since it will probably become increasingly difficult to preserve the river's natural assets amid a rush to new commercial development as the city's tourism industry continues its rapid growth.

In the final analysis, commercial development must be forced to help maintain a delicate balance with the park-like atmosphere that has made San Antonio the most visited city in Texas. To destroy this balance will, in the end, destroy the attraction and allure that brought millions of people to the River Walk and to San Antonio in the first place.

This little winding, unassuming stream should continue to flow with the charm it has always possessed. Its slow moving water should serve to remind us of the gentility harbored between its banks.

THE RIVER WALK IS AN UNRIVALLED SETTING THAT DRAWS CROWDS TO A VARIETY OF ANNUAL EVENTS, FROM COUNTRY MUSIC CELEBRATIONS TO MARDI GRAS FESTIVITIES, TO THE ARTS AND CRAFTS EXHIBITION SEEN HERE. *San Antonio Convention and Visitors Bureau Photo*

Will the message of gentleness it sends regularly to all who will listen remind future generations of what the San Antonio River has meant to so many? Can we preserve the beauty that Edward King, a writer for Scribner's magazine, saw years ago?

'The San Antonio River was a delicious poem written on water, on the loveliest of river beds, from which mosses, ferns, dreamiest greens and faintest crimson, rich opalescent and strong golden hues peep out, making every few yards a waterscape in miniature, an apotheosis of color."

The poet Sidney Lanier admired the river in 1873, saying it was as if "weeping willows kissed the surface."

O. Henry often spoke of the charm of the San Antonio River. But not many addressed the future of the river.

As the city grew quickly in the early 1900's, the river was not considered by many as the romantic place it had been to visitors in the past. Those who were developing businesses along its banks overlooked its real potential.

The question of how one can make the best use of this rich inheritance is a continuing one. During the last decade there have been several proposals to place structures along the San Antonio River that have been opposed and subsequently canceled or modified. No doubt many more proposals will have to be carefully scrutinized in the near future and into the 21st Century. Hopefully, the historical significance of the river will continue to be used as a guide for its future development.

The temptation to exploit the river in the future must be tempered by those who respect and appreciate its history. If we fail to do that, the beauty and tranquility of the river could be lost forever.

EPILOGUE

A persistent question as I wrote these final pages has been: "How would Hugman want to be remembered for his contributions to River Walk development?"

I am certain he did not want a structure named for him. This is based on his remarks in August 1972 when he asked the River Walk Advisory Commission to adopt a policy prohibiting the naming of structures along the River Walk after individuals.

Instead, he suggested that a plaque be placed somewhere on the River Walk naming all who had made significant contributions to the River Walk.

Thus, the question of how he wanted to be remembered cannot be answered with any certainty. But whatever the appropriate recognition, it is clear he would not approve of any kind of structural or symbolic tribute that would detract from the River Walk's unique character.

He wanted the River Walk development to continue with no one individual or group of individuals being singled out. In essence, Hugman suggested that just as much credit should be given to those who preserve the original design concepts as to those who fought to make it a reality.

Another unanswered question aroused my curiosity almost to a point of obsession: "What would Hugman think of the River Walk today?"

I have strolled the River Walk during the quiet morning hours, early evenings, late at night, to try to determine a response to this question. I have sat on benches at various locations along the river and at the Arneson River Theater. I have surveyed the River Walk from bridges and buildings. I have read and reread his presentations, his letters, his memos, and his comments quoted in newspapers. I have talked with his friends, his wife, his daughter, and his son.

Yet even with all that, the question remains unanswered. In the spring of 1982, I attended a sunrise Easter service at the Arneson River Theater by downtown Lutheran Churches. It was a chilly, windy morning. Topcoats and blankets were used by many in the crowd.

Early in the service, the sound of trumpets and then a choir were heard by a number of guests at the nearby Hilton Palacio del Rio Hotel. Some sat on their balconies and observed the proceedings in this unique setting. Near the end of the service, the largest of the Arneson River Theater bells was rung. I heard it echo down the river channel as if the sound would continue forever. Then, it drifted away into silence.

Later, I realized that there was something special about the bells that I had overlooked. Their place had been prepared many years before they were hung. They had been carefully designed for Hugman. Their metals were systematically selected. Hugman was honored with these bells for his contributions to the River Walk. These bells have a singular significance on the River Walk.

IN HIS LATER YEARS, RIVER WALK ARCHITECT ROBERT H.H. HUGMAN CLOSELY MONITORED EVERY NEW CHANGE AND PROJECT ALONG THE RIVER, STRESSING THE NEED TO MAINTAIN ITS HISTORIC STYLE AND TO BALANCE COMMERCIAL DEVELOPMENT WITH NATURAL BEAUTY.

Photo from Mrs. Elene Hugman

Bells have existed from ancient times and today are valued not just for their sound, but for their historical significance and symbolism. They have been used to summon, to proclaim, to warn, and also are musical instruments. The pealing of bells can conjure up images of real or imagined places.

Whenever I hear these particular bells, I will always be reminded of a young architect who had a vision of a River Walk that would maintain the unique, historical character of San Antonio. A poignant reminder of this principle to those who will care for the River Walk in the future is what Hugman wanted most of all!

Thus, a sentence in his final speech has very special significance:

"Perhaps, by the next time you visit Paseo del Rio, the bells will ring for you; yes, and for me, too."

References

1. McCracken, Dick. 1992. "Rip Van River." *The Word*. San Antonio, Texas: Incarnate Word College, Winter, v. 28, pgs. 2-4.

2. Allsbach, Michael. 1993. Telephone interview. (Mr. Allsbach is employed by the Edwards Underground Water District).

3. Lomax, Louise. 1948. *San Antonio's River*. San Antonio, Texas: The Naylor Co.

4. The Edwards Aquifer Authority. 1993. (several publications entitled Edwards Underground Water District).

5. Unidentified newspaper clipping, "Indian Cultures Flourish in Olmos Basin," on file at the DRT Alamo Library, San Antonio, Texas.

6. Hester, Thomas R. 1980. *Digging Into South Texas Prehistory*. San Antonio, Texas: Corona Publishing Co.

7. Teran, Don Domingo. *Itinerary and Daily Account Kept by General Domingo Teran de los Rios into Texas*. Translated and edited by Mattie Austin Hatcher and Paul J. Foik, pt. 3, *Preliminary Studies of the Texas Catholic Historical Society 2* (1933) pp.54-55, in Weniger, Del. 1976. *Wilderness, Farms and Ranch*. Esther Macmillan (Ed.). *San Antonio In The Eighteenth Century*, p. 100, San Antonio, Texas: The San Antonio Bicentennial Heritage Committee, 1976.

8. Espinosa, Fray Isidro de Espinosa, *The Espinosa-Olivares-Aguirre Expedition of 1709: Espinosa's Diary* trans. Gabriel Tous, ibid. 1 (1930): Weniger, Del. 1976 *Wilderness, Farms and Ranch*, in Esther Macmillan (Ed.).*San Antonio In The Eighteenth Century*, p. 102, San Antonio, Texas: The San Antonio Bicentennial Heritage Committee.

9. "St. Anthony Feast Day Observance Set," *The San Antonio Express*, June 12, 1969.

10. Weniger, Del. 1976. *Wilderness, Farms, and Ranch*, in Esther Macmillan (Ed.). *San Antonio In The Eighteenth Century*, pp.99-118. San Antonio, Texas: San Antonio Bicentennial Heritage Committee.

11. Ibid.

12. Schuetz, Mardith K. 1976. *The People of San Antonio: In The Period 1718-1731*. In Esther Macmillan (Ed.). *San Antonio In The Eighteenth Century* pp.73-99. San Antonio, Texas: San Antonio Bicentennial Heritage Committee.

13. Torres, Louis. 1993. *San Antonio Missions*. Tucson, Arizona: Southwestern Parks and Monuments Association.

14. Ramsdell, Charles. 1959. *San Antonio*. Austin, Texas: University of Texas Press.

15. Ables, L. Robert. 1967. "The Second Battle of the Alamo," Southwestern Historical Conservation Society Quarterly, Vol. LXX, No. 3.

16. Lomax, Louise. 1948. *San Antonio's River*. San Antonio, Texas: The Naylor Publishing Co.

17. Almaraz, Felix D. 1993. "Bouchu Labored to Restore Missions," *San Antonio Express-News*, July 18, p. 6L.

18. Winfrey, Dorman H. (Ed.). 1965. *Six Missions of Texas*. Waco, Texas: Texian Press.

19. Amdor, Robert C. & Rock, Rosalind Z. 1993. *Brief Chronology of the San Antonio Missions Since Secularization*. San Antonio, Texas: San Antonio Missions National Historical Park.

20. Minor, Joseph E. & Steinberg, Malcom L. 1968. *A Brief On The Acequias of San Antonio*. San Antonio, Texas: The San Antonio Branch of the Texas Section, American Society of Civil Engineers.

21. Baretta, Jack. 1975. *Acequias*. A speech given Dec. 6 at La Mansion del Rio Hotel to Society of Colonial Wars, San Antonio, Texas: On file at the library of the San Antonio Conservation Society.

22. Heusinger, Edward W. 1951. *A Chronology of Events in San Antonio*. San Antonio, Texas: Standard Printing Co.

23. McLean, Bert. 1924. *The Romance of San Antonio's Water Supply*. San Antonio, Texas: San Antonio Water Supply Co.

24. Ibid.

25. Poyo, Gerald E & Hinojosa, Gilberto M. (Eds). 1991. *Tejano Origins In Eighteenth-Century San Antonio*. Austin, Texas: University of Texas Press for the University of Texas at San Antonio Institute of Texan Cultures.

26. De Leon, Arnoldo. 1982. *The Tejano Community, 1836-1900*. Albuquerque, New Mexico: University of New Mexico Press.

27. Roemer, Ferdinand. 1935. *Roemer's Texas*. San Antonio, Texas: Standard Printing Co.

28. Curtis, Albert. 1955. *Fabulous San Antonio*. San Antonio, Texas: The Naylor Publishing Co.

29. Corner, William. 1890. *San Antonio de Bexar: A Guide and History*. San Antonio, Texas: Bainbridge and Corner. Corner is original source, as in Ramsdell, Charles, 1959. *San Antonio*. Austin, Texas: University of Texas Press.

30. San Antonio Fine Arts Commission, 1993. San Antonio, Texas.

31. Pioneer Flour Mills, 1951. *1851-1951: A Scrapbook of Pictures and Events in San Antonio During the Last 100 Years.* San Antonio, Texas: Naylor Press.

32. *The San Antonio Daily Express,* 1887. "The San Antonio River," Sunday, Aug. 23. (author unknown).

33. *The San Antonio Light.* June 30, 1929.

34. *San Antonio Express.* June 29, 1929.

35. Interview with Anne Hugman Robinson.

36. Interview with Mrs. Robert Hugman.

37. *San Antonio Express.* October 18, 1929.

38. *The San Antonio Light.* October 18, 1929.

39. *San Antonio Evening News.* April 27, 1938.

40. *The San Antonio Light.* April 28, 1938.

41. *San Antonio Express.* May 22, 1938.

42. *San Antonio Evening News.* September 15, 1938.

43. *The San Antonio Light.* October 30, 1938.

44. *San Antonio Express.* October 30, 1938.

45. *San Antonio Express.* December 16, 1938.

46. Interview with Robert H. Turk.

47. *San Antonio Express.* June 14, 1939.

48. *San Antonio Express.* September 17, 1939.

49. Wilkinson, Pam. 1977. "The River of River Cities." *San Antonio* magazine, September, pp. 42-47.

50. Interview with Frank W. Phelps.

51. Interview with Joe Aycock.

52. Crane, Carl J., records submitted by Mrs. Crane in June, 1982.

53. Hugman, Robert H.H. 1966. Letter dated April 11 on file in the library of the San Antonio Conservation Society, San Antonio, Texas.

54. Gunn, Clare K.; Reed, David J., and Couch, Robert E. 1972. *Cultural Benefits from Metropolitan River Recreation — San Antonio Prototype.* Technical Report No. 43. Texas Water Resource Institute, June, College Station, Texas: Texas A&M University.

55. Telephone interviews with Mrs. David Jones.

56. Interview with Mr. Walter Schultze.

57. Greenberg, Mike. 1982. *San Antonio Express-News,* April 14.

58. *River Walk Policy Guidelines.* 1989. City of San Antonio: City Council Ordinance No. 69351 adopted April, 27, 1989.

59. Allen, Keith. 1993. Interviews with Keith Allen of the U.S. Army Corps of Engineers in summer of 1993.

60. San Antonio River Conceptual Plans published by the City of San Antonio and the San Antonio River Authority. 1993: *San Antonio River: Conceptual Plan for Guenther Street to Espada Dam. San Antonio River: Conceptual Plan for Nueva Street to U.S. Highway 281.*

INDEX